THE ROAR

God's Sound in a Raging World

Bob Hazlett

Future Coaching Publications

The Roar by Bob Hazlett
Published by Future Coaching Publications

Special quantity discounts for bulk purchase are available for sales
promotions, premiums, fundraising and educational needs. For details write:

Future Coaching Publications
P.O. Box 2067
New Haven, CT 06521
Email info@bobhazlett.org

Scripture quotations mark NKJV are from the New King James Version of
the Bible. Copyright © 1979, 1980, 1982 by Thomas Nelson, Inc., publishers.
Used by permission.
Scripture quotations marked NIV are from the Holy Bible, New International
Version. Copyright © 1973,1978,1984, International Bible Society. Used by
permission.

Cover design by Web Vision Graphics, www.webvisiongraphics.com

Library of Congress Cataloging-in-Publication Data:
An application to register this book for cataloging has been submitted to the
Library of Congress.
International Standard Book Number: 978-0-9896134-0-8

First Edition
Printed in the United States of America

Bob Hazlett is one of the Church's undiscovered gifts. He has an international ministry, but his gifting has yet to be discovered by many. Bob is one of my favorite prophetic ministers, and he has had a very important role in my life, as well as in the life of the ministry of Global Awakening. We invite him to speak at our Global School of Supernatural Ministry every year, and his teaching has a deep impact on our students. His new book is a very helpful and encouraging work on the prophetic. It is an easy read, an inspiring read, and an edifying read. I highly recommend it to all.

Randy Clark
Senior Leader
Global Awakening

Bob Hazlett's powerful new book, *The Roar*, is more than a book; it's a Holy Spirit journey into the very heart of God Himself. Bob unearths the roar of God's voice that calls us to extravagant intimacy and continual communion. This book could radically alter your walk with God, taking you from the outer court of a boring existence to the holy place of divine encounters. I highly recommend this book.

Kris Vallotton
Senior Associate Leader, Bethel Church, Redding, CA
Co-Founder of Bethel School of Supernatural Ministry

I have hardly ever met a prophetic person like Bob Hazlett, a man who loves the church, understands the heart of God, and is knowledgable in introducing the prophetic as a lifestyle. The Vineyard Movement in Germany, Austria, and Switzerland wants to develop a prophetic culture where churches and individuals understand the importance of the prophetic. Bob Hazlett is our trainer and mentor, but most of all a dear friend who is supporting us on our journey in a wonderful way.

This book is an inspiration to those would love to learn to hear God in the context of today's spiritual challenges. Bob helps us understand God better in His desire to share His plan with us. You will learn to hear, listen, apply and share God's inspiration in an acceptable and healthy way. I hope that all the members of our Vineyard churches in Germany, Austria, and Switzerland will read and apply what Bob Hazlett has written.

Martin Buehlmann
Leader of the Vineyard Movement in
Germany, Austria, and Switzerland

More than ever before, the world needs the word of the Lord as well as His presence and His power. God wants to speak to His people. Even more, He longs for His children to hear His voice. He will speak to any open heart or through anyone willing to carry His word to others. None are more used in this assignment than His prophets.

We are in a day when some of what claims to be "prophetic" is actually quite "pathetic." Scripture documents that this unfortunate reality is not new. In response, God never allows us to "throw the baby out with the bath water." Instead, He teaches us to study His word and discern His voice. He gives us those who are gifted, those who are the real deal. These are people who operate in their gifts and calling with honesty, humility, and a genuine love for God and His people. Bob Hazlett is one of those individuals. The integrity of his motives, coupled by the wisdom of his methods, allows God to use him in a fresh and unique way.

As his Pastor and Bishop since 2003, I have seen Bob's character, his family life, and his gifting grow. He has refused to settle for the old wine or the superficial. I've watched him submit to spiritual authority while never surrendering his own God-given uniqueness and personal convictions. I have seen his love for the people as opposite to a warped kind of love for the stage. He is a servant with the heart of a lion, a rare combination in this day and age.

The Roar is an easy read, but a powerful look into God's heart and mind toward His people. It will be hard for you to put it down once you taste of the insights and perspective that God has given to this man. Practical revelation, for me, is the most powerful revelation. This book is filled with the kind of "God thoughts" that you can download and apply right now and for the rest of your life.

I'm honored to write this endorsement and to have this man serve alongside me here at Kingdom Life Christian Church in Milford, Connecticut. I expect there will be many more books to come.

Bishop Jay Ramirez
Senior Pastor, Founder of
Kingdom Life Christian Church, Milford, CT

Bob Hazlett is a father; a gentle heart with a courageous spirit. This book will shake mediocrity off of your life wherever it is hiding and awaken a deep yearning in you to pursue greater depth and intimacy with Jesus. God is not far away working in disconnected apathy toward a fallen, rebellious people; He is near and longs to draw close to those who have lost their way. *The Roar* is not just another nice read and Bob

Hazlett is not just another prophetic voice. This book is about awakening what God has already placed deep inside of you and it comes from a man who has lived it out. Don't miss this opportunity to dive into the deep end and wade in the water.

Jake Hamilton
Jesus Culture Recording Artist
jakehamiltonmusic.com

Dedication

This book is dedicated to the previous generations that have carried the sound of God in the earth. From Abel to the present day, known and unknown, I am honored to be a watchman over your words.

Acknowledgements

To my best friend, teacher, mentor, and guide. Holy Spirit, thanks for helping me to hear the roar.

To my closest earthly friend, life-long companion, and loving wife. Kim, thanks for being a dreamer and a doer with me. You are amazing!

To all the leaders and friends around the world that have embraced God's sound and encouraged me to be a voice in my generation.

To all the members of the FutureCoaching online community. Thank you for being hearers and doers. Keep running!

To Jeanine and Brian Blount without whom *The Roar* would have remained silenced. Thanks for your tenacity, skill, and creativity.

To a generation yet to emerge. May you hear the sound of deep calling unto deep and respond.

Table of Contents

Foreword by Bill Johnson

The relationship Adam and Eve enjoyed with God in the Garden of Eden was rich in communication. Hearing from God was normal and natural, free of effort or striving. Because this relationship has been restored to us through the blood of Jesus, we can pursue the voice of God, confident of His desire to speak to us.

One of the most basic desires of every believer is to hear God's voice. In fact, Jesus was emphatic about this issue when He said His sheep *know* His voice. God's voice brings life. Hearing His voice is an absolute; it is part of our new nature in Christ and a key element to discovering our purpose in life. Hearing His voice qualifies us for prophetic ministry. Reduced to its most simple component, the prophetic is hearing from God and declaring what He says.

The Roar is a very practical look into the prophetic ministry—a ministry meant for every believer. The author, Bob Hazlett, skillfully brings the abstract and complicated into the open and makes it practical. This book teems with great inspiration and profound insight into the heart of God. When you consider that all life and ministry flow from that place of knowing God's heart, you realize what a treasure you now hold in your hands: a road map of sorts for those longing for more, for those who desire to become all that God intended for them to be.

The Roar contains clear instructions on what it looks like to bring encouragement and life to people who desperately want to hear from God. But it also includes insights on how to speak to those who haven't a clue that God would ever want to speak to them.

To serve God well and represent Jesus accurately, we must see God as He is and rest in our significance in Him. From there, we have the privilege of loving people through God's heart to theirs. This is how we bring life and transformation to many. I have witnessed for many years that the prophetic is one of God's best tools to help people to see God correctly.

This book will awaken or reawaken the intimacy and heart cry to know God. As that cry is opened before the Lord, you will encounter Him as you ponder the glorious role you have been given as a son or daughter of God. In these pages, you will find a loving invitation to experience intimacy and the voice of God.

As a pastor, I am especially drawn to Bob's view and practice of the prophetic. He truly lives to be an encouragement to everyone, empowering people to step into their full potential in God. For us, he is one of the *trusted prophetic voices* right now because he comes as a servant, a true servant of the Lord. I am very thankful for him. He has had a very positive impact on our community of believers.

Bill Johnson
Bethel Church, Redding, CA
Author of When Heaven Invades Earth
and Hosting the Presence

Foreword by Mark Chironna

When we think of God's voice, we often find ourselves with a mixture of metaphors. Sometimes we think of a still small voice. Other times we are mindful of the "sound" of the Lord God walking in Eden in the "cool of the day," which prior to the Fall brought no sense of apprehension to Adam. Yet now after the Fall, that "sound" terrified Adam and he fled from the approaching presence of His Father. Adam had become a lost son, and his lostness affected his hearing in relation to the voice of the Lord. The profound alienation that is the result of the Fall and sin didn't simply disconnect Adam from God, it disconnected Adam with and within himself, and also alienated him relationally with others, and even with his ability to rule over the work of God's hands in Creation. That profound alienation, that lostness, is seen in all its devastating reality by the way Adam, God's lost son, responds to the "sound" (the Hebrew *qol* speaks of something like a roar and something thunderous) of God's Presence—the "voice" that calls out looking for and asking him to be able to answer the question, "Where are you?"

Adam couldn't readily admit where he was because in the Fall he lost his sense of *who* he was. Identity is destiny. Apart from the Father's presence, we are like Peter Pan and his friends in Neverland, living on the Island of Lost Boys (and Girls). So alienated had humanity become from God the Father that when Christ enters the final weeks prior to His ultimate sacrifice at Calvary, He cries out,

> *"Now is my soul troubled. And what shall I say? 'Father, save me from this hour'? But for this purpose I have come to this hour. Father, glorify your name." Then a*

voice came from heaven: "I have glorified it, and I will glorify it again."

The Son of God is going to taste death, taste that profound alienation from His Father and from all that the Fall caused lost sons to experience, in order to restore us to fellowship with His Father.

In crying out, the Father responds from Heaven. Yet the degree of "lostness" and alienation in the bystanders is revealed by how they responded to what they heard. Jesus heard His Father, the rest heard it this way:

> *The crowd that stood there and heard it said that it had thundered. Others said, "An angel has spoken to him." Jesus answered, "This voice has come for your sake, not mine. Now is the judgment of this world; now will the ruler of this world be cast out. And I, when I am lifted up from the earth, will draw all people to myself."*

The crowd couldn't discern the voice of the Father because they were alienated from Him.

What Jesus heard clearly as His Father, He says came for their sakes to indicate that the prince of this world who had profoundly impacted their ability to hear, see, and be intimate with their Father, would be cast out. Some heard that voice as thunder, others heard it as perhaps the voice of an angel. Regardless, in this instance, the voice was anything but still and small. It was authoritative, it was established, and it was majestic. It had a lot of reverb in it, if you will. It was the voice of a Father who finally had a Son who knew who He was, where He was going, and what He was to accomplish.

The cry of the Father in the beginning after the Fall, "Where are you?" is now answered by the Son, who because He knows who He is in His Father says, "Here I am," without hiding in fear or shame. This amazing and intimate bond of love between the Father and the Son reveals the Father's will and intent for every lost child of His. That sound that frightened Adam after the Fall actually drew him near prior to the Fall.

How far we have fallen from enjoying the "sound" of the Father's voice. We live in an hour when there is a deep in the saints (placed there by God in our spirits) that has the capacity to respond to the depths in God. How that is possible that mere humans have the capacity to comprehend the depths of God is still a mystery to me. Yet, what an awesome privilege and thrill!

Bob Hazlett, a dear and precious friend and, more importantly, a key voice in this hour, is inviting you to go on a journey as you read *The Roar*. Let his journey inspire yours. It is time for sons and daughters to respond to the voice of the Father and share His love with the nations until the whole earth is filled with His glory. The Lion of Judah is roaring in a company of sons and daughters who are once again walking with their Father in the "cool," or literally in the Hebrew, "the Spirit," of the day. Let Bob Hazlett awaken in you the yearning that God placed there, and learn the prophetic pulse of the voice of your Father, and walk in the rhythm and cadence of heaven by continually drawing near to Him every time you hear Him roar.

Mark Chironna MA, PhD
Mark Chironna Ministries
Church On The Living Edge
Orlando, FL

INTRODUCTION

"The best book is not one that informs merely, but one
that stirs the reader up to inform himself."

—A.W. Tozer, Man the Dwelling Place of God

Introduction

When all that generation had been gathered to their fathers, another generation arose after them who did not know the Lord nor the work which He had done for Israel.

~ *Judges 2:10 (NKJV)*

In every generation, God allows new voices to emerge. God has used people to carry His sound in the earth throughout history. The prophets reminded people what God had done and gave them hope for what God was about to do. Their goal was not only to record history and release destiny, it was to create an environment where people could know God by observing His activity and understanding His heart.

I was privileged to grow up in a home where talking about God and His activity was commonplace. I am also grateful to live in a generation that has been preceded by great leaders who have reminded us who God is by revealing His words and His activity through prophetic ministry. Prophetic ministry should be a fresh voice and not an echo. Different streams and schools of prophecy all add dimension to God's voice. The Holy Spirit teaches us each in a unique way.

My hope is that, as I share what I have learned, you too will be taught by the Spirit and become a unique voice for God in this generation. I honor the giants of the faith, known and unknown, whose shoulders I stand upon. The reason I am writing this book and the volumes to follow is to help a new generation to be taught by the Spirit and find their voice.

Jesus and Cheesesteaks

On my fourteenth birthday, my parents presented me with a gift, a book by A.W. Tozer entitled *The Pursuit of God*. I was definitely more excited about their second gift, a *Sports Illustrated* magazine subscription. Having grown up in the Philadelphia area, I am passionate about two things: cheesesteaks and complaining about my sports teams. The Phillies were in the pennant race that year, and the Eagles were solid contenders in football playoffs. Being a Philadelphia sports fan is a continual exercise in the exhilarating quest to win the big game accompanied by the frustrating reality that we rarely do. Needless to say, the last thing on my mind was reading a book by a guy who, by the look of his picture, wasn't a passionate enthusiast of anything, except maybe libraries. I have come to realize that A.W. Tozer is perhaps one of the most passionate pursuers of God that has ever lived.

One night, I surprised myself by picking up Tozer instead of the sports magazine. There is not much that can move a fourteen-year-old boy to tears unless his team loses the big game or his cheese falls off his steak sandwich. However, when I read *The Pursuit of God,* something stirred deep within me. As I read the first chapter, "Following Hard after God," I was gripped by the awareness that God is passionately pursuing me, and His pursuit stirs a passionate response in me.

 @bob_hazlett

"To have found God and still to pursue Him is the soul's paradox of love." —A.W. Tozer. Keep running after Him!

Over the decades since, I have returned to that book many times. I have yet to read the whole thing through at one time, and it is not because the writer lacked passion. Rather, the opposite is true. Every time I read that first chapter, it creates

the same effect it did back then. I become a pile of mush in the presence of God. Just the mention of Tozer sometimes makes me teary eyed. He followed hard after God, and now, years after his death, he still inspires me to do the same.

I get excited about hearing God and helping others enter conversation with Him. I am a student and a teacher of prophetic ministry, and that is the topic of this book. However, any exploration of God's sound has to start with a pursuit of His heart—a lesson I learned from Tozer. To pursue the roar of God's voice without taking the time to chase after His heart is to miss the point entirely.

Prophetic people are first people of God's presence. Without His presence, we are more likely to be speaking from our own head than His heart. We have to know Him in order to sound like Him. To speak God's words without knowing His heart is like eating a cheesesteak without the cheese or the steak—empty! Paul said it in these words: "If I have the gift of prophecy . . . but have not love, I am nothing" (1 Cor. 13:2, NIV).

When we experience God's love, it causes us to long for God's heart and pursue His presence even more. Then God meets us and stirs an even greater hunger within us. This phenomenon was demonstrated in another passionate pursuer of God, David. He didn't just chase God, he ran fervently after God's heart. Psalm 42 is a description of that pursuit. Many scholars believe this was written by David and performed by the Sons of Korah. They were kind of an ancient Hebrew boy band that led worship in the temple. David longed to be in God's presence. For those of you offended by my comparison of spiritual hunger to a carb-loaded, grease-filled sandwich, David paints an even less appetizing picture in Psalm 42.

Licking Your Own Wounds

"My tears have been my food day and night" (Ps. 42:3, NIV). That's a pretty sorry picture. If you take a moment to read the whole psalm, you'll find that David was at an absolutely destitute point in life. He was despondent and longing for God's presence. He described his soul as downcast and in turmoil within him. And it wasn't David alone who is wondering. The people around him repeatedly questioned David about whether God was even with him any more. This was worse than losing a big game; he felt labeled as a big loser.

It seemed like God was nowhere to be found, and that created a thirst in David. It was a thirst so extreme that it had him eating his own tears and licking his own wounds. Do that for very long and you will have a thirst even Gatorade can't quench! "As the deer pants for streams of water, so my soul pants for you," David cried (Ps. 42:1, NIV).

God doesn't know how to think small. Everything He does is over the top. Not only did God hear David's cry, he responded in an amazing way. David asked to be refreshed by a sip from a stream. However, God's answer came to him in a deluge. "Deep calls to deep in the *roar* of your waterspout," David wrote. "All your breakers and your rolling waves have swept over me" (Ps. 42:7).

God responds to us the same way He did to David millennia ago—extravagantly! Ask God for a sip and He will answer you with a tsunami. Ask Him for refreshing, and He will let you drink from a fire hydrant. Our over-the-top God loves to meet us in our deepest moments of darkness and pour out His presence, grace, and provision in remarkable ways.

If You Are Disturbed, That's Normal

David was disturbed in his soul because it seemed God was not there. Actually, it was the closeness of God that was causing the disturbance. As Tozer so eloquently argued, it is God's passionate pursuit of us that stirs hunger in us for more of Him. God disturbed David to bring him even closer than he was already. God initiated the pursuit. God initiated the sound. His deep called out to David's deep.

God is not bothered by us being bothered. He is not upset that we get upset. He is not disturbed when we are disturbed, even with Him. I believe He is the one stirring the atmosphere around you, drawing you into His presence.

My hope is that this book will inspire you in the same way that Tozer and David inspired me. I hope this book disturbs you. I hope it hits you in that deep spot. I want you to hunger to be hungrier and thirst to be thirstier. I want you to be passionate about pursuing and communicating with God. I hope you become hungrier for God's heart, God's sound, and maybe even Philly cheesesteaks. I want you to hear the roar!

CHAPTER 1
GOD'S SOUND CREATES

"O God, I have tasted Thy goodness, and it has both satisfied me and made me thirsty for more. I am painfully conscious of my need for further grace. I am ashamed of my lack of desire. O God, the Triune God, I want to want Thee; I long to be filled with longing; I thirst to be made more thirsty still. Show me Thy glory, I pray Thee, so that I may know Thee indeed. Begin in mercy a new work of love within me. Say to my soul, 'Rise up my love, my fair one, and come away.' Then give me grace to rise and follow Thee up from this misty lowland where I have wandered so long."

—A.W. Tozer, The Pursuit of God

God's Sound Creates

What God Sounds Like

God is in the communication business. He always has been. I am a student and teacher of prophecy and prophetic gifts, so communication with God is a topic I enjoy. However, this book is not just about prophecy, and it is not only for those who aspire to prophetic gifts. God is building a communications company, a generation who communes and communicates with Him. God raises new voices in every generation. However, we live in a time when God is raising an entire generation with a new voice! This will be a prophetic company going about the Father's business.

I believe the best way to tell any story is from the beginning. If you want to learn how God sounds, you should go to the source. There are hundreds of Old Testament examples of how God speaks through men and women. There is also great instruction and understanding in the New Testament about prophecy. We should have an understanding of both. This book will focus on how God and mankind communicated in the beginning. Jesus came "to seek and to save what was lost" (Luke 19:10, NIV). He came to restore our original value and relationship with God. This book will explore the ancient sound of God, how it was lost, and what it sounds like today.

He Called Me Son

Words have power. One word has the power to change a life. If you believe the Genesis account of creation as I do, all that we see began from one word: "light."

There was a moment when one word changed my life. It was the mid-1990s, and life was going pretty well for me. I was a pastor, and ministry had been successful and fulfilling. Around that time, people kept telling me about a revival going on in Pensacola, Florida, and urging me to go check it out.

I don't know what the word *revival* means to you, but I grew up around such events. To me, it brought a picture of super-excited people becoming super emotional and dancing around. I was not against that, but I had been there and done that—or so I thought. I was skeptical, but I decided to check it out anyway.

What I found in Pensacola was super-excited people becoming super emotional and dancing around, but they were also genuinely encountering God and genuinely happy. They were happy to line up at 6 A.M. in the Florida summer sun. They were happy to stand, worship, pray, and get to know one another until 6 P.M. when the doors opened. By that time, the line looked almost one mile long. I don't know what you would call that. I think the word *revival* works.

The first night I stood in the back thinking, "These people are much too happy for church people." Unfortunately, my perspective at the time was that serving God was hard work with little reward, and God was mostly disappointed with our efforts. On the second night, someone found out that I was a pastor and put me in front in the pastor's section. I was telling myself this was a good thing until I realized I was right in the middle of the flag wavers.

I don't know if you have ever been to a meeting like that—I had not. I enjoy exuberant worship now, but at the time it disturbed me a little. Nearly being hit by flailing arms and flopping flags was not my idea of church. Sometimes God has to disturb you in order to get your attention. He has to offend your old idea in order to give you a new one. I had picked an aisle seat

for quick escape if necessary only to find that I was pinned in by an ocean of flying flags. No escape!

Trying my hardest to ignore the flag waving, I concentrated on worship. Just when I was really getting into the lyrics of one of the songs—"Let your glory fall in this room, let it go forth from here to the nations"—the pastor interrupted the song.

"There's a preacher here tonight," the pastor began.

Inside my head, the thought occurred to me that there were many preachers there that night. There was a whole section of us sitting right there in front. Just as quickly as that cynical thought crossed my mind, another thought came from outside my head: "He's talking to you."

I listened as he continued. "You were standing in the back last night, criticizing this revival." Well, maybe he was talking to me. "But God wants you to know that He brought you to the front tonight because He's going to change you."

His words shifted to a first-person perspective. "Son, I am going to use you to . . . " There was a lot more that he said, but I missed the rest because something inside of me began to break open. I was no longer hearing the words of a preacher, but that of a Father. I began to weep, and I am not a weeper.

I cried so much that I walked out to gain my composure, and I sat down in the back hallway to get my wits back. I was telling myself, "I'm *not* the preacher he was talking about, and that word was *not* for me."

Just then a woman approached. She looked intently at me and said, "You *are* the preacher. That word was for you!"

One word can change your life. It was not the vastness of the promises that impacted me, but the personal nature in which God spoke. He called me son.

I believe God's sound, His roar, is not primarily to tell us what to do, or correct us from doing wrong. His voice comes to tell us who we are and to empower us to do what we were created to do. His sound sometimes has to be dramatic to get our attention when the raging noise of the world overcomes our ability to hear. The skeptical sounds in our heads and the chaotic sounds around us drown out His voice. I am glad God is not shy. If He has to, He will roar! All you have to hear is one word, and it will change your life.

I realized something that night that is true for all of us. God's sound is not so much about a special calling or a great destiny to touch the nations. It is that we all carry a special identity. He called me son. When you hear God's sound, it gives you permission and power to become who God says you are. He doesn't just want to take you to your dream; He wants to teach you who you are. God knows that if you go to the nations but don't know who you are, you can lose your identity out there. If you build a great business and base your identity on it, you gain nothing. If you go out on the streets and see lots of amazing healings and miracles but aren't grounded in sonship, you miss the most important point. When you realize that the greatest title you can possess is not prophet, performer, millionaire, or minister, you will embrace your greatest identity: to be a son or daughter of God.

God's Hovering Presence

In the beginning God created the heavens and the earth. Now the earth was formless and empty, darkness was over the surface of the deep, and the Spirit of God was hovering over the waters. And God said . . .
~ Genesis 1:1-3 (NIV)

This book is about God's sound. The sound of His voice is how He created the earth. Genesis has always been one of my favorite books of the Bible. It displays God's original intent for man and the created world. It is full of stories of God's exploits, and it clearly demonstrates God's desire to partner with us relationally to accomplish His purposes on the earth. Just as I learned that night in Pensacola, the book of Genesis reminds us that our true identity and destiny is to be sons of God, created in His image and likeness.

Genesis begins with the creation story. The opening verses paint a picture of the setting in which God chose to focus His creation. It depicts the state of the earth in the womb of God's creation. This version of the earth was a prehistoric, muddled mess with infinite potential because it was coming from the imagination of an infinitely good and loving God. The earth was described as formless, empty, chaotic, and full of darkness. Yet it is also described as deep. It was a raging, hot mess, but God saw the roar of potential in it. This was potential contained within the earth's embryonic state because it was a potential birthed out of God.

This earth was then the focus of two purposeful actions by the Creator: He hovered and He spoke. The Spirit of God hovered over the waters. It's an intimate picture that displays a cultivating presence charging the atmosphere with creative potential.

 @bob_hazlett

God's principles taught outside of experience with God's presence & power may produce results but will rarely reproduce people who know God.

God wasn't far away, orchestrating His creative genius in a removed, remote, detached manner. He also was not being an over-protective helicopter parent, trying to guard the earth or keep it in a shielded environment. It's the same way in your life. God's Spirit hovers and moves to initiate His plan. He draws close to your chaos and dwells in it, just as His deep touched the earth's deep. His presence is what conceives the possibilities of what you can become.

The word *hover* is used again in Deuteronomy 32:11 where it is also used to describe God's loving presence. He is likened to "an eagle that stirs up its nest and hovers over its young, that spreads its wings to catch them and carries them on its pinions." The hovering action of the mother eagle stirs up the infant birds, allowing them to be carried away by the mother. This is how they learn to fly. This is the same picture of God's care described in Genesis 1. The Spirit of God hovered over the waters, and His Spirit stirred up the possibilities created by His presence.

God's Spirit continues to hover over His creation, infusing it with the potential for a creative miracle. The great worshipper-king David knew this hovering presence well. In Psalm 42, David describes a similar picture of God's deep presence interacting with His creation. David, in the midst a time of personal despair, intimately described God's activity in this way: "deep calls unto deep in the roar of your waterfalls" (Ps. 42:7, NIV). This imagery echoes the creation story. Deep light is calling forth unto the deep darkness of the waters.

"The Bereshit Rabba," an ancient rabbinical interpretation of Genesis, makes this note about the condition of earth before creation:

> *On the passage, "And the earth was empty and formless" (Gen. i. 2), our Sages remark as follows: "The words tohu and bohu mean mourning and crying; the earth mourned and cried on account of her evil lot."* [i]

Creation was crying out for the sound of God. The apostle Paul, a rabbi himself, was well aware of this understanding of the creation account when he wrote the words, "We know that the whole creation has been groaning" (Rom. 8:22, NIV). Paul was referring to the raging sound of a waiting world. What is the world waiting for? "The creation waits in eager expectation for the sons of God to be revealed" (Rom. 8:19, NIV). Just as the primitive earth cried out for the sound of God, today's earth cries out to hear the sound of God's children. That roar comes from relationship with God. According to Paul, this is the sound of sonship. "The Spirit you received brought about your adoption to sonship. And by him we cry, 'Abba, Father'" (Rom. 8:15, NIV).

Similar to the groaning of the earth, David was crying out for more of God. His turmoil was evident throughout that psalm. Yet that pain doesn't end in hopelessness. He reminded himself to put his hope in God. He hungered and thirsted after God's presence just as desperately as a parched deer longs for the refreshing of a stream of water. He knew that his downcast soul was hopeless without the refreshing touch of God's Spirit. He also knew that God never disappoints.

Just as God's Spirit was the one hovering over the earth and stirring the waters in the opening scene of creation, so also it was God's Spirit who was stirring the hunger within David. Deep need was intimately stirred by deep, creative power. Deep hunger and thirst was initiated by God's deep, overwhelming presence. David thought he was the one crying out to God when actually it was the Spirit's hovering activity that was charging the environment with the potential for a miracle.

God's desire for us hovers over our lives and stirs us up to a place of hungering after Him. He meets us and satisfies our need, but it is a thirst that is never quenched. We are satisfied but never contented. Deep continues to call out to deep.

Tornadoes, Waterfalls, and Waterspouts

I was always a kid who loved learning, but I was easily bored. I just couldn't sit still long enough, and I couldn't focus on just one activity well. In sixth grade, my teacher moved my desk next to hers to help me concentrate better, but it didn't work out well because my constant fidgeting frustrated her.

She wasn't the only one frustrated. So was I—until I walked into Mr. Mercier's eighth grade math class. He took advantage of every holiday or special occasion to dress up and teach us math principles with costumes, crazy glasses, and memorable stories. My favorite was the math assassin story, "Artie Chokes Two for a Dollar at the Grocery Store." It was in Mr. Mercier's class that I realized I learned best through stories and pictures. He made math so enjoyable that I took honors math all the way to calculus. Passionate people are contagious.

God knows I learn best through pictures, and that is how He often speaks to me. The way I learn affects the way I teach. I think in pictures, so I teach in stories.

I had one of those pictures one night while worshipping God. I didn't ask for it, it just came. I saw a picture of a dense cloud form. As I watched, it turned into what looked like a tornado. It was like watching a 3D version of a weatherman's animation screen, but someone else was controlling the graphics.

The tornado moved over a body of water and sucked the water into it, forming a waterspout. The two merged into one body and then moved all over dry land, pouring out water over the parched terrain. Vegetation started growing where the land had been barren before.

I knew this vision was from God, and I responded the way I usually respond when God speaks to me: "Huh?" I was totally confused. I didn't have a clue what the picture meant.

I find that when God speaks, He often leaves us questioning. Then when we ask questions, He usually doesn't answer the questions we think He should answer. Instead, He initiates communication in order to create an environment in which we ask the questions that He really wants to answer. He doesn't always give the answer we want. He does give us the one we need. Prophetic experiences are, by nature, ambiguous. I am convinced God is not looking for a monologue; He is seeking a dialogue. He draws us closer into relationship with Him as He speaks to us. He starts the conversation, and He hooks us into asking the questions that lead us to His heart.

"What is that?" I asked as I was bewildered by the vision of the waterspout.

The answer came quietly in my heart: "It is deep calling to deep."

Now I was even more puzzled. Deep calling to deep? What did that mean?

Some people think interpreting God's symbolic language requires profound spiritual intuition. Not really—it's easy if you have the right phone app. My Bible and a biblical language program led me to Psalm 42:7. I read the familiar psalm with totally new eyes! This was David's psalm about God meeting him in his time of greatest need. "As deep calls to deep, in the *roar* of your waterfall [*waterspout*] all your waves and breakers sweep over me." As I studied the words, I realized two things: that *waterfall* and *waterspout* can be used interchangeably in this context, and that the *roar* of the waterfall is the same word used for God's voice in Genesis!

I started studying more about waterspouts. They are akin to a tornado that forms over a body of water. I learned that the pressure created by the cloud forms the waterspout. As it touches down in water, the water is sucked up into the spout. Eventually the water of the cloud and the water from the surface become so intermingled that you can't distinguish the two. What is in the cloud goes into the water, and what's in the water goes into the cloud. The substance of the cloud becomes one with the substance of the body of water. I've heard the idiom "raining cats and dogs," but as a waterspout eventually moves over dry land, the cloud can literally rain fish and frogs!

This is what God was showing me when He said it's a picture of deep calling to deep. As God calls out to us, it stirs something within us that calls back out to Him. His presence comes and infuses our lives in such a way that we are a part of Him and He is a part of us. Eventually, through constant communion in and with His presence, it becomes impossible to distinguish between what is us and what is God.

God was showing me a prophetic picture of how we go deeper in the Spirit—through communion. That communion, impacts everything we touch. When we become one with Him, we rain heaven on earth.

Like David, throughout our lives we all find ourselves in situations in which we are crying out for more. That cry is stirred by God's hovering presence, just like the cloud hovering over the body of water; it exerts pressure and eventually forms a waterspout. As we cry out for more of Him, He responds with an overflow of His presence. He comes into us as we are united with Him.

Many people miss God's activity of His deep calling to their deep. They cry out for more, and they think more is an outpouring or a miracle. They are expecting God to do something *for* them. Instead, He desires to do something *in* them. More is a communion. More is union with Christ. More is Him dwelling in you and you dwelling in Him. More is His deep calling to your deep.

It's not enough to be refreshed by God's presence so that we can go back to life as usual. We have to be transformed by His hovering, creative presence. As we become the people who

God has destined us to be in Him, we find the longings of our hearts fulfilled. But watch out! Just when you think you are satisfied, God's Spirit hovers again and stirs a greater hunger for even more.

God's Voice Is a Roar

Have you ever been to Niagara Falls? The sound there is amazing. The roar of the waterfall creates a persistent, resonating rumble that thunders for great distances. This is the imagery used in Psalm 42 to describe God's activity. "Deep calls to deep in the *roar* of your waterfalls."

Once again, the depiction of God's presence as a roar shows us how extravagant He is in His desire to be in communion with us. He could have trickled or sprinkled or sputtered. David would have likely been satisfied with that. We, too, often settle for much less than what God desires for us. Even if we may become contented with less, God isn't satisfied with giving us sufficient provision to satiate our need for Him. He goes overboard, because that's the kind of God He is. Offering hope or joy or peace isn't enough for Him. He desires to give us Himself. He gives so much that it has us crying out for more—the more of communion. Rather than trickling, the waterfall of God's presence thunders through our lives as a roar.

 @bob_hazlett

God is extravagant in His responses. When you thirst for Him like a stream, He answers you with a waterfall! Amazing! Psalm 42

As I researched the word *roar*, I learned the Hebrew word used there is *qol*, which can be translated as roar, voice, sound, or noise. It is found in many instances in the Old Testament, but I was amazed to learn that its first occurrence is in Genesis shortly after the creation story, after Adam and Eve fell into sin.

*Then the man and his wife heard the **sound** of the Lord God as he was walking in the garden in the cool of the day, and they hid from the Lord God among the trees of the garden. But the Lord God called to the man, "Where are you?"*

~ *Genesis 3:8-9 (NIV)*

It was the sound of God's voice that called out to Adam and Eve during their darkest moment in the same way that the roar of the waterfall came to David during his darkest moment. Adam and Eve had never known such desperation because prior to the Fall, they had been in continual communion with God. In that moment, the sound—the roar—of God called out to them. He didn't want to just ease their pain; He was calling them back into His presence.

Like Adam and Eve and David, we find ourselves in times of darkness. Our need for rescue, as extreme as it may seem to us, pales in comparison to God's desire to draw near to us and to commune with us. His deep is calling out to our deep, bridging the divide between us and drawing us into His presence like a waterspout.

God's sound beckons us, and God's sound also contains power. Waterfalls and waterspouts are images of immense force. His voice doesn't just sound like something; His voice *does* something. His voice creates.

The Roar + Relationship = Prophecy

In the opening lines of Scripture, the Spirit of God hovered over the surface of the deep, and then God spoke. The simple act of speaking released what was inside of Him into existence. Speaking made the invisible visible. His voice put substance around His desires. When God said, "Let there be light," the light that was within Him became tangible as it took on a material form. God continues to create in this way today.

As we respond to God's roar in our own lives and we join in communion with Him, we become people of His presence. He dwells in us and we dwell in Him. As we live in relationship with the Creator, we learn to hear and respond to God's voice. He enjoys speaking to us, and when we give voice to His words, He continues His creative work.

Prophecy gets a bad rap because people over-complicate it or misunderstand it. At times, prophecy can even be misused because it's not held within the context of love. It's not an overly mystical, highly unattainable skill reserved for the elite. Prophecy is as simple as hearing what God says and saying it. It is a by-product of relationship with God.

When you are in relationship with people, communication is part of the relationship. God likes to talk! If we listen, He often has things to say that will release His destiny and purposes into people's lives or circumstances. As His deep calls to our deep, the roar of His voice continues to create change in the earth. He speaks, and as we speak what we hear, His words do what they have always done—they bring light to darkness, resources to emptiness, and order to chaos. They roar in a raging world!

CHAPTER 2
GOD'S SOUND
CAUSES CHANGE

"All nature has come to expect from God a sense of orderliness. Whatever God does carries with it His fingerprint. And in the world around us His fingerprint of orderliness is evident to anybody who is honest with the facts. If you look at nature, you will discover a mathematical exactness. Without this precision, the entire world would be in utter confusion."

—A.W. Tozer, And He Dwelt Among Us:
Teachings from the Gospel of John

God's Sound Causes Change

Fries and the Roar

I learned early in my childhood that God speaks to people. I grew up in church and had an amazing pastor who seemed to talk with God all the time. Sometimes, right in the middle of a really great point in his sermon, he would stop. He would look up to the left and say, "Yes, God. I hear you. All right, God. I'll do that." I never knew what my pastor was hearing, how God could speak so clearly to him, or why God was always up and to the left.

When I was fifteen, I got my first job at a Chick-Fil-A in a mall. My boss told me that my job was to make the french fries. Easy enough, I thought. Then my boss added, "It's the hardest job here, and you better not mess it up."

He went on to explain that the french fries have a shelf life of two and a half minutes. If they aren't served within that time, they are dead and have to be thrown out. This is complicated by the fact that people also don't like to wait for their food, and if the customers aren't happy, the boss isn't happy. I didn't want people waiting for their food, nor did I want to be responsible for the death of three-minute-old fries!

I hoped to do the job right, but I also had no idea how to time the fry cooking. Then I thought about my pastor. God spoke to him while he worked. Maybe God would speak to me while I worked too. So I prayed and asked God to speak to me about the fries.

A little while later, I had this impression that I should start making some fries. I looked around and didn't see any customers, nor was anyone near the food court. The longer I stood looking at absolutely no one, the stronger the impression came that I *really* needed to start up some fries. I didn't know if that was God speaking to me or not, but I went with it and loaded up the fryer. Two and a half minutes later, just after I pulled the large batch of fries out of the oil and salted them, a crowd hit the restaurant. There was a fry rush that lasted over two hours!

When my boss saw that crowd coming, he was shocked that I was ready with the fries. Not only that, but I kept up with the crowd all day long. After my shift was over, my boss declared, "We're going to make you the fry master! You're the best fry maker we've ever had!" And then he gave me a raise.

Jesus never wanted to become uninvolved in our lives. Sin damaged our relationship with God, but it was always His intention that we walk in communion with Him. That's why He came to earth and died for us, to restore us back into communion with Him.

God wants to be intimately involved in every area of our lives. He has things to speak and potentials to be released through fellowship with us. He wants to talk to us about what is important to us, even about french fries! As we commune with God and meditate on what He says, His words have meaning. They will bring about His purposes. Joshua 1:8 (NIV) states,

> *Keep this Book of the Law always on your lips; meditate on it day and night, so that you may be careful to do everything written in it. Then you will be prosperous and successful.*

He wants to be involved in our lives. He is the greatest teacher, mentor, creator, and communicator. Why would we not want Him to speak to us? He has great ideas! His deep is calling out to our deep in a roar. He calls out in our most vulnerable

moments like David in Psalm 42, but He also calls out in situations we usually leave Him out of, like making french fries.

So What Happened at Creation?

In Genesis 1:2, we read that the earth was formless, empty, and dark. God's Spirit hovered, and then He spoke creative order into being. He loved the earth so much that He refused to let it stay in its formless, empty, dark state. The world was raging, but the roar of His voice changed everything in an instant.

The best starting point in learning to hear God's sound is where it all started, in the beginning. We should not reduce God's voice to a spiritual gift or a special calling reserved for specific people. God always has and still does desire to speak to all of us. His voice is relational and transformational. He could have chosen any number of methods to create, but He chose to do so through sound. Our job is to hear His sound and respond to it.

God is still in the business of creation. He is still transforming the formless, empty, and dark places. His words have power, and His words bring life. As we learn to listen to them, they turn chaos into order, emptiness into resources, and darkness into light. They set things right.

Chaos to Order

My grandma loved to knit. When I was a child, she lived in a little apartment in the back of our house. She would spend hours knitting in her rocking chair. I loved being with her and watching her creativity as she made something beautiful from a simple ball of yarn.

My favorite part about her hobby was when she got to the end of a yarn ball. "Give me your hands," she would say. I would extend my arms in front of me, and she would start wrapping the thread around my hands. Then she would take her time to carefully wind that yarn into perfect little spheres that she could use to easily knit.

Sometimes my brother and I would sneak to her yarn basket late at night and roll the balls back and forth. Eventually, as a result of our messing with the balls and her endless knitting, the balls would start to unravel and become tangled. The different colors and textures all mixed together in a jumble of knots, and the yarn became absolutely useless. She would give me the tedious job of separating them and putting them back into orderly balls again. Once again that basket would be filled with perfectly ordered, colorful balls of yarn.

 @bob_hazlett

A powerful effect of hearing God's voice and speaking His words is U and God will spend time together to bring order 2 the chaos around U.

The primordial earth was similar to my grandma's basket of yarn when it was at its worst. It was chaotic. God's voice spoke into the chaos and brought order to it.

I enjoy studying scientific topics and discovering the intersections between science and spirituality. I often find nuggets of God's truths in the most unexpected places, like when I came across the term *entropy*. It comes from the second law of thermodynamics, which states that an object left on its own without being acted upon by outside forces will lose order. It will break down, lose energy, and deteriorate. Entropy is a measure of the disorder in an object.[ii] Like my grandmother's yarn balls, God's created order will fall into disorder unless someone or something applies energy to it. Without an outside force supplying energy, entropy always wins.

The good news is that our God isn't satisfied sitting on the sidelines and letting us become a casualty to entropy. He is the outside force that brings order to our chaos. God's roar decimates entropy. At creation, His voice ripped through the chaos and ravaged it with His purposes in an instant. It roared!

Our world is filled with formless disorder. War, famine, divorce, crime, addiction, social injustices, and poverty are all examples of entropy gone unchecked. Chaos abounds, but one word spoken from God's heart can change the entropy in a second.

What God Didn't Say

When I was younger, I didn't always have an appreciation for a tidy bedroom. I often cleaned by hiding everything in the closet. When my room was particularly bad, Dad used the word *squalor*. I'm not sure exactly what it meant, but I'm pretty sure it resembles "now I must judge you!"

The truth is that sometimes we find ourselves in squalor. Whether because of our own choices or the circumstances around us, our lives can become a mess. But God's voice doesn't resound with judgment. Rather, His voice brings order to the chaos.

Several years ago, I was in a hotel room preparing to speak at an evening session of a conference. I was simply spending time with God as I happened to look out the hotel window to the pool. It was empty at the time, but I saw a distinct picture in my imagination. I would call it a vision.

The picture I saw was of a young man from the conference. He stepped into the pool and walked from the shallow end into the deep water. He kept walking until he was fully immersed.

I didn't know what it meant, but I tucked the image away in my mind. Several hours later, I was surprised to see the exact man I had seen in my imagination attending the conference. I struck up a conversation with him and told him about the vision I had earlier in the day. He thanked me with a smile, and we both went our separate ways.

At the end of the service that evening, I felt particularly impressed to ask if anyone wanted to give their lives to Jesus for the first time. I was a little taken back by this impression—after all, we were at a Christian conference. But I went with that fleeting thought and asked if anyone wanted to give their lives to Jesus.

To my surprise, the same man I had seen in the vision of the pool came to the front and dedicated his life to God for the first time. "Can I be baptized in the hotel pool tonight?" he asked. I was elated! Late that night, after the service, we got permission from the hotel manager to baptize the man in the hotel pool. He was fully immersed in the water, just as I had seen earlier.

The next day, I had an opportunity to spend some time with that young man. I asked him what his spiritual journey looked like. "I've heard a lot about Jesus, but I grew up in a faith in which we worshipped and prayed to many gods. Jesus was one of them." He went on to explain that during the evening service a light bulb went on for him. He realized that Jesus was the unique Son of God and it was time for him to follow Christ only.

As I reflected on this event later, I asked the Holy Spirit a question. Why did I see a picture of him being baptized in the pool and not a picture of him worshipping many gods? His answer stunned me: "I could only show him to you as I see him, and I created him to be my child. When you saw what I see about him and said what I say about him, he became what I created him to be."

God's words reveal His heart. What He doesn't say is just as important as what He does say. God didn't pronounce His judgment on that man's idolatry. Rather, His words spoke into being His purposes for the young man.

When God hovered over the formless, empty, dark earth, He didn't declare, "What a mess!" He didn't start pointing out all the issues that were wrong with the earth's state. Rather, He spoke destiny and released what the earth could be through His words.

 @bob_hazlett

You can shift conversations from negative to positive with your words. Be positive.

God's words spoken through us can do the same thing. That is the essence of prophecy. When we hear God's voice, it transforms us. When we speak His words out, they change the environments around us. Prophecy brings God's order through words. It reverses entropy. One word, *son*, changed me in a moment through that pastor in Pensacola. One prophetic word changed the young man at the conference forever as well. In the same way, one word from God's creative genius spoken through your mouth can instantly bring chaos to order in someone else's life. Our role as prophetic people who hear God's voice is not to identify the problems around us but to release the solutions.

Emptiness to Resources

Not only does God transform the formless into order, He fills emptiness with resources. At creation, God transformed an empty earth into one filled with God's desires: "Let there be light!" Then there was light. Soon after, God's words further filled the earth with land and sea, fish and fowl, trees and tarantulas, and man and woman.

I was around eleven years old when I was in a Bible class at church. The teacher asked us what we wanted to do when we grew up. All the usual answers were delivered: a doctor, a teacher, a policeman, and a nurse. When my turn came, I spontaneously blurted out, "I want to marry a pastor's daughter with blond hair and blue eyes!"

I'm not sure who was more shocked, me or everyone else in the room. Why would I have said something like that? I chastised myself. It all seemed very strange until ten years later when I stood in another church and watched a blue-eyed, blond-haired pastor's daughter walk down the aisle to marry me. I had spoken what God had revealed to me, and the words birthed the reality. An empty spot in my life was filled by my wife, and it was God's words which spoke that into being.

Words carry intentions. God's words reveal what He intends to do. Whatever He does, He first speaks. He desires to fill the empty voids in peoples' lives with Himself. He can do that through a scripture, an inner voice, a dream, or a million other means. But He also loves to speak through us. He actually likes us! He truly enjoys doing things with us! His creative activity is no exception. He loves partnering with us to fill the earth with His presence.

The power of prophecy doesn't lie in magical words. The power of prophecy is in God's presence. When we speak God's words, they release the presence and power of God to accomplish what He said He would do. It is God who fills the emptiness, and He often chooses to do it with His words spoken through our mouths.

Lack of Vision

Emptiness can take on many forms. Financial, emotional, relational, and spiritual lacks are all manifestations of the emptiness around us. Sometimes what is lacking is opportunity or strategy. God's words speak those things into existence. One prophetic word of wisdom can allow you to see God's purposes in your circumstances and how you can get from where you are to where you are called to be.

One form of emptiness is a lack of vision and understanding of God's plan for our lives. Proverbs 29:18 (KJV) states it this way: "Where there is no vision, the people perish." It's heartbreaking to live without vision or purpose. Prophecy can reveal God's plans which give vision and direction for people's lives.

I once had the privilege of speaking with a soccer player named Nicola. I gave him a prophetic word that he would play for the national soccer team, score a winning goal, and give testimony on national television about God's work in his life. That television interview would spark enough notoriety to write a book about his experiences and encourage young people to pursue success while living morally pure.

What I didn't know was that Nicola's soccer career was mediocre. He was a reserve player who spent much of his time sitting on the bench. He also wasn't the youngest guy on the soccer field, and his years were catching up with him. He was discouraged that it seemed his athletic career might be coming to an end. There seemed to be an emptiness of any form of opportunity for this man.

He could have shrugged off my prophetic word, but instead Nicola believed what God said and began training hard. If he was going to play on the national team, he had to be prepared.

He did everything he could on his end to be ready when the time came for the prophetic word to become reality.

Eventually, he got a phone call. A player on the national team had been injured and they needed him to stand in. When game time came, he was ready. The first quarter passed, then the second, and then the third. The game was entering the final minutes, and he was still sitting on the bench.

Nicola's team was in the lead when he finally got called onto the field to play. In a surprising move, the opposing team managed to tie the score. In a last-minute maneuver, Nicola stole the ball and took it down the field for a game-winning goal! The exhilaration of that moment was soon intensified as television reporters crowded around him for an interview. Just as God said, Nicola spoke about God and living a pure life right on national television.

His career didn't end there. He continued to train hard, play with excellence, and live a pure life. Eventually he wrote a book about his experiences in which he encouraged young people to pursue success while also upholding their moral standards.

What Nicola accomplished was completely unimaginable without God's one word roaring into the void. That word transformed the situation and placed vision and opportunity into a place that seemed destitute. Ephesians 1:3 tells us that God has blessed us in the heavenly realms with every spiritual blessing in Christ. His purposes and blessings are already a reality in the heavenly realms. He desires to release that potential into substance that we can experience here on earth. This reminds me of Jesus' prayer that God's will be done on earth as it is in heaven.

Sometimes, a prophetic word is released that reveals heaven's purpose. That revelation simultaneously sheds light on two things: God's intentions and the things that are lacking in order for those intentions to be fulfilled. When Nicola received the word about playing on the national team, he realized there was much work to be done to become prepared for the moment when that opportunity to play on the national team materialized. When he acted upon what God had spoken, he was able to walk into the destiny God had for him because he had completed the prerequisites that are necessary for the word to come to pass.

In the same way, sometimes people are not walking in all the things God purposed for them because they aren't willing to fulfill the prerequisites necessary to walk in their destiny. God may have spoken that you are to be a teacher of the Bible who enlightens Scripture to bring people closer into relationship with Jesus. That is an amazing destiny! However, God's purposes to partner with you in that endeavor will never come to pass if you never open your Bible and begin to learn it and integrate it into your own life. In order to be transformed by the Word, you must become the Word.

Darkness to Light

Dark is scary. It holds hidden dangers. You can get lost in the dark. When I was a kid, my window curtains were decorated with the helmets of my favorite sports team. I loved looking at them during the day and imagining what it would be like to one day wear one of those helmets as a player on that team. But what was a comfort during the day became terrifying at night. The helmets morphed into fearful shapes, and sometimes they even had voices. Darkness can be very deceiving.

Not only does the darkness distort reality, but danger also lurks in the dark. Harmless children's toys turn into lethal weapons when stepped on in the dark. Walls jump out from nowhere! Even in the familiarity of my own home, I have been known to lose my sense of direction in the dark and end up nursing a head wound during a middle of the night bathroom run.

Other sorts of darkness abound in our world. Many people find themselves lost in the distortion of a dark period in their lives. Darkness lies to us and offers us a twisted view of reality. Instead of confidence, there's uncertainty. Instead of clarity, there's distortion. Instead of purpose, there's disorientation.

When God saw the darkness in Genesis 1, He spoke to it. He said, "Let there be light," which literally translated states, "Light in me, be!" What was inside of God was the solution to the darkness. His own essence brought about light. Prophecy does the same thing. Prophecy is much less about what or when or why. It's about whom—Jesus!

The disciples had trouble with this concept. Sometimes I think Jesus messed with them on purpose. He spoke in riddles and analogies that left their heads spinning. But afterward, something special would happen. They would pull Jesus aside and say, "I don't get it! What do you mean?"

Jesus knew they wouldn't get it. The point of the conversation was equally to teach them something and also to draw them into His presence. He wanted them to seek Him as much as He wanted to impart an understanding. It was communion that was of highest importance.

One such occasion is found in John 13-14. Jesus said something really mysterious, and the disciples were left bewildered. Here's a rundown of the conversation:

Jesus: "I'm going somewhere you can't come."

Peter: "Where are you going?"

Jesus: "Don't worry, guys! I'm going to prepare a place for you in my Father's house. You know the way to get there."

Thomas: "Um, Jesus? We aren't even sure where you are going. How can you say we know the way to get there when we don't even know what you're talking about!"

Jesus: "I am the way, the truth, and the life. No one comes to the Father except through me."

The disciples wanted an answer to the same question many of us have: What is my future and how do I get there? It's a question that is programmed into us from eternity. We all have that gut-level intuition that we must be here for a greater purpose. It's a God-given agitation that is designed for one purpose: to lead us to Him. The disciples wanted to know how to step into their destiny, and Jesus' response was that He was the way.

 @bob_hazlett

God rarely answers the questions we want Him to. He usually creates a scenario that causes us to ask Him the question He wants to answer.

Darkness is terrifying, but Jesus brings light. When we lose our sense of direction, He is the way. When the clouds of deception mar our views of reality, He is the truth. When danger lurks in hidden places, He is the life.

Prophetic words spoken from God's heart through us can destroy the darkness that reigns over people's lives. As we speak the words God wants us to speak, it will bring light into their darkness. Jesus is the way, the truth, and the life through their dark times.

Prophecy Shows the Way

One of the most frustrating experiences I occasionally have is getting lost in an unfamiliar city. Good thing I have a GPS. Whenever I don't know where I am, where I'm going, or how to get there, the little voice in my GPS always figures it out. Just as my GPS can tell me, "Continue for three miles" or "Make a U-turn now," likewise prophecy can bring confirmation or correction to the paths we are on.

I was recently speaking with a woman when I had an impression for her and her husband. I told her I saw her husband getting a new job. It would move her closer to their children, and it would also provide a better work schedule to accommodate more family time. She shared with me that her husband was a doctor and that they had recently moved from a different part of the country so he could take a new position at a hospital. They had decided to move so they could be closer to their children and grandchild and so her husband could have better hours. However, they had been unsure that they were on the correct path. This prophetic word was a confirmation to them that they were following God's desires for their lives, and it brought great comfort to her.

Prophecy Reveals the Truth

During moments of darkness, it becomes easy to accept things as truth that are really only shadows. Deception lurks in darkness. Prophecy functions as a light bulb to bring truth to the situation, and suddenly the distorted shadows are revealed for what they are.

Several years ago, a minor physical ailment was troubling me. I had tried everything I knew for quite a long while, and yet the problem persisted. Having run out of every option I could find to resolve the issue, I became convinced this was a spiritual

battle. I asked trusted friends to pray diligently with me in defeating this demonic attack against my body.

One of my friends mentioned an impression he received when he prayed for me. He sensed that I should stop eating a certain food. Could it be that simple? No demons? No spiritual warfare? Sure enough, I stopped eating that food and the problem disappeared. I was in darkness about what I should do, but one prophetic word shed light on the situation and brought about a healing in my body.

Prophecy Brings Life

Darkness conceals very real dangers. John 10:10 tells us that the thief comes to steal, kill, and destroy, but Jesus comes to bring us life. God's words released over us will lead us deeper into the life that God has planned for us. The devil is cruel and wicked and determined to do anything to rob us of that life. Prophecy can bring understanding to a situation that the enemy designed for our destruction. Though crafted for maximum danger, these obstacles turn into a mere nuisance when handled God's way.

I once was speaking to a businessman and felt impressed to tell him that I saw him in a legal dispute. A business partner was threatening to drain his financial resources and rob him of years of work. I told him if he let God be his lawyer, the case would be settled and he would not lose.

He told me it was true that there was a legal problem with a partner. Because of the prophetic word, he changed his legal strategy, and the dispute was settled very quickly and without great loss. While the situation could have devastated this man financially and professionally, the resolution allowed him to make a new start and build his business even stronger than before.

Become and Release

The earth is still filled with chaos, lack, and darkness. But we also have raging areas of disorder in our own lives as well. We remain in a tension of being saved but also needing to be saved. When we hear God's voice, it releases His creative power to move us off the path of darkness and into our destiny. He calls us "son," and we become what God says we are. God wants you to first become and then release His Word into the environment around you to change it.

One of my online Future Coaching students recently shared a testimony with me. God had been doing some amazing things in her, teaching her and stretching her into new things prophetically. She wanted to grow in prophetic gifting, so she chose to exercise hearing God's heart for others as she went about her day.

She was window-shopping at a boutique when she sensed God saying to her that the store wasn't named correctly. She wasn't sure what to do about that, but she asked God how she could help this business become what God saw it being. She walked around the store asking God what His purposes were for the store. She decided to strike up a conversation with the owner, and she expressed encouragement and care as they had easy dialogue about the business and products in the store.

Prophecy isn't as complicated as people can make it out to be. It's simply encouragement, comfort, and edification from the Holy Spirit. This lady was building a bridge of encouragement that made it easy to share what God had to say about the business.

Eventually the student asked, "Have you ever thought about changing the name of your store?"

"Actually," the owner replied, "I was considering that earlier this week. Sales have been down lately, and the name was one of the things I was thinking about changing." They started talking more about what a name change might be, and the owner became excited at the prospect of what a new name might do for the business. She was so encouraged by the conversation that the two ladies brainstormed a new name and even developed a logo that incorporated the owner's favorite colors.

The businesswoman was encouraged by the interaction, and she had hope once again that her business could flourish. God's voice transformed the business, and the businesswoman may have never even known it was a prophetic word from God. There was no churchy language or "Thus saith the Lord." No one played a worship song or said a long prayer. Rather, it was just two women talking together, but one of them had a secret. She was speaking God's words. Those words were bringing order to chaos, resources to emptiness, and light to darkness.

CHAPTER 3
GOD'S SOUND
OUT OF YOU

"Nothing is complete in itself but requires something outside itself in order to exist."

—A.W. Tozer, The Knowledge of the Holy

God's Sound out of You

First Things First

Any conversation on prophecy must begin with relationship. Sure, there are models and tools that are useful in growing in prophetic ministry, but these must always be secondary to relationship. At the core of prophecy is learning how to hear God's voice. You can't do that without valuing relationship with Him.

As I started my personal journey in growing in the prophetic, the first thing God taught me was how to have a personal relationship with the Holy Spirit. This was awkward to me in the beginning. I had grown up honoring the Father and Son, but I didn't know much about the Holy Spirit. We called Him the Holy Ghost in my church. That conjured up scary images of an inaccessible, phantom-like figure. I also knew that the Holy Spirit leads us to the Father and Jesus, so I had a distorted impression that I wasn't supposed to worship Him. And I certainly didn't want to talk to Him for fear that I might accidentally blaspheme Him and never be forgiven!

Then I started to realize that my views of the Holy Spirit didn't line up with what Jesus said about Him. In John 14-16, Jesus describes the Holy Spirit as our comforter and mentor. He is a guide who leads us to truth.

When I picked up a biography of Kathryn Kuhlman, I was intrigued by the way she interacted with the Holy Spirit. She spoke of Him as her best friend and described how she would wait on His presence before she began a meeting, no matter how long that took. She would talk to Him while in bed, sometimes using a foreign language.

A sense of longing began to stir in me for more of the Holy Spirit. In September of 1997, I prayed, "Holy Spirit, I want to learn what it is like to be your friend." I didn't really know what to expect, but I knew I needed to know Him better.

 @bob_hazlett

If God is the last person U talk to before U go to sleep & the first person U hang out with in the morning, it's hard to have a bad day!

What I didn't anticipate was having to give up football. For two seasons, I found myself sitting down to enjoy a game on television when the Holy Spirit would interrupt my favorite pastime. On one such occasion, I was wrapped up in the game and my team was winning when I heard the Spirit say, "Let's take a walk."

"Now?" I asked, feeling a little peeved.

"They're going to lose, and you're not going to like it," He said.

As soon as I started walking down the driveway, the Holy Spirit encountered me. I experienced His presence with and on me. I felt enveloped and embraced, like being hugged by the Holy Spirit. There were no words, just an overwhelming expression of His presence. We walked together for an hour. I cried the entire time, thanking Him for His presence.

In the years since, I have learned how to treasure my relationship with the Holy Spirit. He's the first person I speak to in the morning and the last person I speak to at night. I've learned that many of my initial perceptions of Him were wrong. Rather than being mysterious, scary, and timid, I have found through my encounters with Him that He is talkative, personal, and hilarious!

New Ways of Communicating

Two things happened in me as I developed a relationship with the Holy Spirit. First, the Bible came alive to me in a new way. The Holy Spirit illuminated scripture to me. It's much easier to understand the Bible when the one who authored it provides a running commentary about it. Some people fear that valuing the Holy Spirit means devaluing the Word of God. I've found the opposite to be true. As I walk in relationship with the Holy Spirit, He brings understanding and appreciation of the scriptures that I didn't have before. Not only does He enable me to understand the scriptures, He empowers me to become them. The scriptures transform me.

Second, as I grew in relationship with the Holy Spirit, my prayer life changed. I don't even use the word *prayer* often any more. I just talk with God. I hang out with Him and listen to what He has to say throughout my day. It's a two-way conversation in which we listen and respond to each other.

I love spending time with my wife. In order to keep our relationship strong, we enjoy setting aside times to be together and listen to each other. Coffee dates are one of our favorite ways to really connect on a heart-to-heart level. But we also have constant communication outside our set coffee dates. Even when I'm on the road, we regularly check on each other through phone calls, texts, and Skype.

In the same way, there are two ways I spend time talking with God. One is a conscious communication in which I take time to say, "God, I'm focusing my heart on you now." I make myself aware of His presence. I use those times to pray scriptures, pray for other people, or pray God's proclamations over my life. The second way I talk with God is in continual communication. As I go about my day, I'm always interacting with Him.

I'm often asked how a person can grow in prophetic gifting. Over the years, I've learned many valuable lessons about the mechanics of prophecy, but I've learned them all through relationship with the Holy Spirit. First Corinthians 12 tells us that there is one Holy Spirit but many manifestations of gifts from the Holy Spirit. The key to operating in any spiritual gift, including prophecy, is to cultivate relationship with the Spirit who gives the gifts.

Designed to Hear the Holy Spirit

Hearing God's voice can be overly mystified. Sometimes people expect hearing God's voice will involve out-of-body experiences, frightening encounters with angels, or an audible booming message. All of those things can happen, and there are examples of each in the Bible, but hearing God is often much more simple than that. Just as you and I do, God communicates in many different ways. When I want to talk to one of my friends, I can go to their house in person, call them on the phone, set a lunch appointment, send a text or private message, or choose from any number of methods. In the same way, God loves to talk to us, and He will find lots of ways to do it. It may be through a vision, a dream, a voice heard internally, or just an inner knowing. I have found the more I respond and interact with the first thing I hear Him say, the further He converses with me.

Another misconception is that if we open ourselves to hear the Holy Spirit, we also open ourselves up to hearing other voices, some of them demonic. In John 10:3-5 (NIV), Jesus addresses this issue and likens us to sheep and Himself to a shepherd:

> *The sheep listen to his [the shepherd's] voice. He calls his own sheep by name and leads them out. When he has brought out all his own, he goes on ahead of them, and his sheep follow him because they know his voice. But*

*they will never follow a stranger; in fact, they will run
away from him because they do not recognize a
stranger's voice.*

Several reassurances are found in this passage. First, the
sheep know the shepherd's voice. Just as every child can isolate
their parent's voice in a crowd, so also you can hear your
Father's voice. You were born for this! You are His son or
daughter. From the foundations of the earth, you were created
to recognize and respond to God's voice.

Second, we are promised that we will not follow the voice
of a stranger. We aren't promised that there will be no other
voices. Sometimes God's voice gets drowned out in our own
inner dialogue, the schemes of our enemy, the conflicting voices
of other people, and the cares of life. But the assurance is that
we are wired to hear God's voice and that when we do, we will
follow it. The Holy Spirit will lead you and show you which
voices belong to a stranger and which belong to God.

This also applies to prophecy. Since prophecy is just an
extension of hearing God—hearing God for others—you are
designed for prophecy as well! In fact, on the day of Pentecost,
Peter declared that what happened that day was a fulfillment of
promises foretold by the prophet Joel.

*In the last days, God says, I will pour out my Spirit on all
people. Your sons and daughters will prophesy, your
young men will see visions, your old men will dream
dreams.*

~ Acts 2:17 (NIV)

Astoundingly, this passage tells us that the Spirit of God
was poured out on all people, and all people will prophesy.
Prophecy isn't reserved for the spiritual special forces. It's not
just for the guy with a big ministry and title. If you possess the
title son or daughter, you are called to prophesy.

Prophecy involves encouragement, edification, and comfort (1 Cor. 14:3). In other words, prophecy is good news. If someone hears some good news, what do they do? They smile! We tend to overcomplicate prophecy. There are really only three steps involved: God speaks, we listen, and we say what He said. Part of the over-complication of prophecy comes through how we communicate it to people. Just because we are speaking God's words doesn't mean we have to say, "I have a word from God for you." Statements like that can be alarming at best and offensive at worst. I like to simplify things by saying, "Can I share something that will make you smile?" God's words to people are encouraging, so we need to make sure the way we communicate them is also encouraging.

One of the online Future Coaching participants recently shared a story about an experience he had when he asked God to speak a word of encouragement for someone around him. He was in an airport on a layover, and he stopped at a restaurant to grab a meal between flights. As he ate his salad, he prayed, "God, I want to grow in hearing your words for other people. Would you show me someone you want to speak to?"

Immediately, his attention was drawn to a TSA airport security agent sitting at a table nearby. He got an impression that this agent was going to counsel young women and give godly advice for their lives. He felt like this message was from God, but he was unsure how to open the topic with the agent. As he walked toward the woman, he noticed that she was reading a book about finding life purpose in God, so he felt emboldened.

He approached the woman, excused himself for interrupting her dinner, and said, "This may sound strange, but I'm a Christian and I believe that God can speak to me. May I share something with you that I think will be an encouragement?" The woman was surprised but also wanted to hear the encouragement, so he continued. "I see God using you to bring counsel and wisdom to young women. Does that make sense to you?"

The woman put down her book and replied, "Yes! Thank you for sharing that! Just this week I was asked by my church to begin counseling young women. I wasn't sure if that was what God wanted me to do or not. But because you shared that encouragement, I now know that this is truly what God wants me to do."

God Likes to Tell Secrets

Have you ever had a secret that was so good that you just had to let it out? Sometimes a secret is too exciting to keep to yourself, like when you have a special gift to give to a loved one. God has lots of good gifts to give, and He doesn't like to keep the secrets to Himself.

Amos 3:7 (NRSV) tells us, "Surely the Lord God does nothing, without revealing his secret to his servants the prophets." God's desires and plans within Him want to get out. The roar of His voice is the means He chooses to turn His desires into reality. The way He chooses to speak is through His people. When we become of voice of God, we reveal His plan and we create with Him.

This verse provides several insights about how God works on the earth. First, He has a plan. He's not an arbitrary, removed God who sits on the sidelines of eternity to watch how our endgame turns out. He has intentions that involve His heart and His divine timing. In other words, prophecy always produces God's desired outcome. Prophecy reflects God's heart and intentions. It's not really prophecy if it's not coming from God's heart. I can say all day long, "In Jesus' name, the cat is a dog," but unless God wants the cat to be a dog, it will still meow.

Second, Amos 3:7 demonstrates that God reveals His plans. He can't keep His own secrets! He still creates through words, so when He wants to do something, it must be spoken. When we speak God's intentions through prophetic words, we are representing God' s heart because we are simply repeating what God said. It's not presumption on our part to speak what God said. Rather, it was His intention from the beginning to speak His incarnational words through our mouths. His word becomes flesh for others to see.

Third, we learn in Amos 3:7 that the ones God speaks to are His servants. He looks for people whom He can trust with His secrets, and He calls them "my servants, the prophets." This reveals the character of the people God chooses to speak to: they are servants. Jesus told His followers if they wanted to be great leaders in the kingdom, they had to be great servants to the kingdom. The first job description of one who hears from God for others is to be a servant.

Servants clean up messes; they don't create or expose them. Prophecy does not primarily involve pointing out problems. Rather, prophecy points out the potential in a person or situation. When we position ourselves to serve, we are also positioning ourselves to hear God. Many of the prophetic words I receive for others as I go about my day come from a posture of wanting to serve. If I go around looking for a prophetic word, I often miss the heart behind God's words. However, if I seek to love people and serve them, it becomes easier to hear God's heart for them.

Amos tells us the people God reveals His secrets to are the prophets. *Prophet* sounds like a big word, and it is. While there are some especially gifted people who can be considered prophets, most of us fall in the category of "all your sons and daughters will prophesy" described in Acts 2:17. We can all hear from God and tell people what He is saying, even though we are not all prophets.

God is looking for people who will listen to His intentions, look for moments to serve others, and live for the opportunity to share what God says. As we partner with God to speak His words, spiritual, relational, and material emptiness will be filled with God's life and power.

Prophecy and Mint Chocolate Chip Ice Cream

When you like to do something, you do it a lot. Every habit starts with a discipline, so choose your habits well. I like mint chocolate chip ice cream. It conjures up old memories of late night conversations with my dad with a big bowl of the creamy dessert. That excitement for mint chocolate chip ice cream spilled over to my daughters as I raised them to have the same appreciation for it that I do.

 @bob_hazlett

If you come to God with a petition you may wonder what the answer is, but if you come to Him for His presence the answer is always YES!

The reason I like mint chocolate chip ice cream has less to do with the flavor and more to do with how much I enjoyed eating it with my dad and enjoy eating it with my girls. I eagerly desire it! God tells us to treat spiritual gifts like mint chocolate chip ice cream. First Corinthians 14:1 (NIV) instructs us to "follow the way of love and eagerly desire spiritual gifts, especially prophecy." When you like something a lot you become passionate about it. When you are passionate about something, you devote a lot of yourself to it and you become good at it. An examination of unusually gifted individuals in any profession—sports, business, the arts—will demonstrate that they are usually also the most passionate. Passion produces giftedness.

The Holy Spirit is passionate about spiritual gifts, especially prophecy. He wants you to get excited about it too. When God tells us to eagerly desire spiritual gifts, especially prophecy, it's not because He's dangling an unattainable carrot in front of us. Rather, He is excited about it, and He wants us to get excited about it also. Just like my dad shared mint chocolate chip ice cream with me and I share it with my daughters, the Holy Spirit wants to grant us our desires for His gifts. He wants us to enjoy communication with our Father. He plants the seed of desire in us, but we are the ones who have the responsibility to cultivate that desire to partner with the Holy Spirit in His ministry of speaking God's words to a chaotic world. Not only does God give you the option of participating with Him in prophetic ministry, He urges you to eagerly desire it!

The Roar of Passion

I have a confession. I talk to myself—a lot. I wasn't aware I did that until recently when my daughter was driving with me in the car. She stopped me and asked, "Dad who are you talking to?"

Her words brought me back to the present. I told her I was talking to someone that I would see that night at the meeting we were driving to. I told her that I was having a vision. I was talking to a woman and telling her she would write a screenplay for a movie, and God would use it to heal a nation in Asia. My daughter looked intently at me and replied, "Whatever." In her language that means, "That is so awesome, and you are so amazing that I don't have words to describe it," or something like that.

The woman I saw in my vision was at the meeting. I repeated to her what I had said in the car. It turned out she had just started writing a screenplay that week. She was greatly

encouraged by the words I spoke. I was greatly encouraged that God talks to me even when I talk to myself and that I can drive and have visions at the same time!

A spiritual vision is a mental image of what God intends the future to be. One of my favorite scriptures is Proverbs 29:18 (NKJV)— "Where there is no revelation, people cast off restraint." Some translations substitute the word *vision* for *revelation*. I like the word *revelation* better in that context. Vision is when you think big; revelation is when you think beyond what has ever been thought before. I like this dictionary definition of revelation: "a dramatic disclosure of something not previously known or realized."[iii]

In the beginning, God created the earth. The word *create* is the Hebrew word *bara*, which means to create substance *ex nihilo*, out of nothing. That requires more than just the ability to see. It requires the ability to see what has never been seen before. That's the kind of seeing God does.

Paul prayed for the Ephesians that God "may give you the Spirit of wisdom and revelation, so that you may know him better . . . in order that you may know the hope to which he has called you" (Eph. 1:17-18, NIV). When we come to God for relationship, He rewards us with revelation. This revelation is a vision that we have never seen before of Him, ourselves, our future, and our calling.

However, before you can have vision for change you must have passion for change. It is true that without vision people cast off restraint, but it is also true that without passion people will never receive a vision. Passion can come from three sources: pain, promise, and people.

Pain Produces Passion

I used to run home from school to watch re-runs of old cartoons. One of the cartoons I loved to watch was *Popeye*. Popeye was a skinny sailor man who always stood up for his girl, Olive Oyl. To be honest, I am not sure what he saw in her; she was not that attractive. Who knows! Maybe he had a vision. The other character in this cartoon was Brutus, the burly guy who tormented Popeye and attempted to steal Olive Oyl away. Then Popeye would reach his boiling point. His face would get red, steam would come out of his ears, and he would say, "That's all I can standz, and I can't standz no more!" Then he would pop open a can of spinach, grow big muscles, and pummel Brutus. That is a picture of passion.

When you can't stand the present, you will have passion to do something about it. Moses was born during a time when nothing ever changed except to get worse. His people had been in slavery over 400 years, and they could not imagine anything else. No one had a vision for the future of Israel. Moses did not even have a vision for his own future. Then one day, something rose up inside him that instigated change. He could not stand it any more.

> *One day, after Moses had grown up, he went out to where his own people were and watched them at their hard labor. He saw an Egyptian beating a Hebrew, one of his own people. Glancing this way and that and seeing no one, he killed the Egyptian and hid him in the sand.*
> *~ Exodus 2:11-12 (NIV)*

Moses was born to be a deliverer, even though he did not know it. In fact, he didn't even know if he was an Egyptian or an Israelite. He did not have the identity or authority to match his passion, but his passion eventually led him to the place where he developed identity and authority. He had to flee for his life, but

when he returned, he came back with a new identity, a rod of authority, and vision for a nation. Passion will lead you to vision.

When something bothers you, it may be something you are called to change. Passion will bring you to the boiling point in which you will move past the place of human strength into the supernatural. Prophetic people must be passionate.

I have a passion to see people move into the future God intends for them. I do not like it when they are stuck. Different gifts have different passions. An apostle is passionate about transformation. A pastor is passionate for community. A teacher is passionate about maturity. An evangelist is passionate about souls. A prophet is passionate about destiny. The destiny of individuals, cities, and nations stirs a passion in prophets. When you find what you are passionate about, you will move past your limitations. It will lead you to your identity and will release great authority.

Promise Produces Passion

Paul's instructions about spiritual gifts are a key to operating in the prophetic: "Follow the way of love and eagerly desire spiritual gifts, especially the gift of prophecy" (1 Cor. 14:1, NIV). I don't know where I heard the following phrase first, but I know I heard it many times growing up in the church: "Seek the giver, not the gifts." I know the intention of people who used this phrase was to inspire people to have relationship with God, but it was accompanied by a chilling effect regarding the pursuit of spiritual gifts. Paul is clear that supernatural gifts require pursuit and pursuit requires passion. Seek both the giver and the gifts. Be especially passionate about prophecy. I like that.

I have spent years traveling and ministering in different cities, states, and nations. Many years I spend more than 250 days away from home. I have stood hundreds of nights for five or six hours as people waited for prayer. Many, many nights I have changed time zones, gone with little sleep, and stayed up very late praying for people. Why do I do this? Maybe it is because I love airplanes and hotels. I don't mind them, but I love being home more. Maybe I'm a night owl and always stay up late. Ask my wife and she will tell you that I am early to bed and early to rise. Maybe I do it because being around people energizes me. The opposite is true. I love people, but if my personality profile is correct, I am an introvert. I get recharged when I am alone.

The reason I do what I do is simple: I get excited to hear about lives that are changed because of God's prophetic promises. Just today, I heard from a family that I prayed for several years ago. I did not remember the encounter, but it was life changing for them. One of the things I said about their youngest child was that he would have a unique learning style and that the education system would try to label him. In that same conversation, I shared some wisdom about how to handle that and how God would use this boy. Now several years later, they are experiencing the exact event. Because I framed their future from God's perspective, what could have been a problem is now a promise. I get passionate when I see God's promises come to pass.

You have to see your promise to maintain your passion. You have to find ways to celebrate even the smallest things. One of the reasons people lose passion is that they lose awe. Celebrate the healing of the hangnail and the headache. Celebrate the small words and the big words. Celebrate every promise fulfilled.

People Produce Passion

Paul ends his discourse about prophecy in 1 Corinthians 14 with these words: "Therefore, my brothers and sisters, be eager to prophesy" (1 Cor. 14:39, NIV). The word *eager* can be

translated as envy. Wow! God is telling us to be envious to prophesy. I am not allowed to envy another person's possessions or calling, but I am allowed to see spiritual gifts in them and say, "I want that too!"

Let me illustrate it this way. If you drive home in a brand new red Ferrari, and I look at your car and say, "I want that car," I am saying I want to take your car from you and put it in my garage. That kind of envy comes from a poverty spirit that thinks if you have a red Ferrari, I can't have one. It says there are a limited amount of red Ferraris available and a limited amount of resources to purchase one.

In God's Kingdom the opposite is true. If I see God do something through someone else, it is an invitation to seek that in my own life. I don't want to take yours. In fact, I want you to have more so I can see what "more" is possible. Unlimited resources are available to us. Jesus said, "I say to you, he who believes in Me, the works that I do he will do also; and greater works than these he will do" (John 14:12, NKJV). This is an invitation to want what He has, and even more is available.

The question could be raised that if it is available for all of us, why do some demonstrate a greater level of operation? If all can prophesy, why are some more effective, more accurate, or more prolific? I believe one of the differences is passion. If you love to do something, you will do it often. If you do it often, you will become good at it.

Malcolm Gladwell in his book *Outliers: The Story of Success* states,

> *The emerging picture from such studies is that ten thousand hours of practice is required to achieve the level of mastery associated with being a world-class expert in anything.[iv]*

Mastery does not seem like an appropriate word when talking about the supernatural, so let's use the word *maturity*. Luke 2:52 (NIV) states, "Jesus grew in wisdom, and stature, and in favor with God and men." Like Jesus, there are some people with special callings and specific assignments. Even a special calling takes growth to achieve maturity.

I remember many years ago being at a series of meetings in which I prayed for every person in the room each night. After the second night, I woke in the morning with very little voice and very little energy. I remember asking God to forgive me for doing His work in my own strength and saying that I would not pray for every person the next night.

That afternoon, I was scheduled to have lunch with a pastor who drove from several hours away to meet with me. As we sat down he said, "God gave me a picture for you today. You were lifting weights and feeling like you were getting weaker, but with each repetition God was adding more weight. Though you felt like you were getting weaker, you were getting stronger. God is developing supernatural strength in your gifts." So much for an early night! I prayed for everyone there that evening. At end of three days, the pastor said, "We have almost 500 individual cassette tapes of prayers for people to pick up." They had recorded each prayer.

Passion will push you past your frustration. Passion will lead you to celebration. Passion will develop supernatural strength in you. Paul said this to his young student Timothy: "I remind you to fan into flame the gift of God, which is in you through the laying on of my hands" (2 Tim. 1:6, NIV). Paul instigated the passion in Timothy, but Timothy had to sustain it. God will use other people to initiate passion in you, but you will have to establish it. Hungry people will stand in line on Sunday to have hands laid on them, but passionate people will wake up Monday and lay hands on others. Passionate people stir up the passion in others. When you are passionate about something, it is hard to keep what is inside from coming out.

Inside God

Everything you see comes from what can't be seen. A tree begins as a seed hidden in the ground. Fruit appears on a vine that looks bare when dormant. A child exists in an unseen form in a mother's womb before being born. Even everyday objects like computers and cars came from someone's idea. It was in their head before it was on your desk or in your driveway.

Colossians 1:16 (NIV) states,

For by him all things were created: things in heaven and on earth, visible and invisible, whether thrones or powers or rulers or authorities; all things have been created through him and for him.

This is also translated in the ASV as,

For in him were all things created, in the heavens and upon the earth, things visible and things invisible . . .

We know that all things were created *by* God and *for* God, and Paul declares they were created *through* God, because they were *in* God. Before anything was created, it existed *in* God. Ephesians 1:4 says, "For he chose us **in him** before the creation of the world" (NIV; emphasis added). You were in Him before you were in the world. You were in Him before there *was* a world. Before God said, "Let there be light," He said, "Let there be you!"

🐦 @bob_hazlett

Hanging out with the Holy Spirit will make your day more enjoyable. Learn to experience "joy in the Holy Spirit." Romans 14:7

Where did this created matter, such as light, come from? I believe it came from the uncreated One. The Bible says God is light; there is no darkness in Him (1 John 1:5). The apostle John describes the process of creation this way:

> *In the beginning was the Word, and the Word was with God, and the Word was God. He was with God in the beginning. Through him all things were made; without him nothing was made that has been made. **In him was life, and that life was the light** of all mankind. The light shines in the darkness, and the darkness has not overcome it.*
>
> ~ *John 1:1-5 (NIV; emphasis added)*

The method that God chose to release what was inside of Him was to speak. The words, "Let there be light" from Genesis 1:3 are properly translated, "Light in me, be." The act of creation was God releasing His presence, His power, and His potential through His words. If it's in your heart, eventually you will say it. Luke 6:45 (NIV) says, "For the mouth speaks what the heart is full of."

Inside You

Paul, in talking to a group of his Colossian disciples, refers to a hidden truth that was to be revealed in us: "Christ in you, the hope of glory" (Col. 1:27, NIV).

When Christ came into the earth, the fullness of God dwelt in Him in bodily form. The presence, power, and potential of God lived in human form. The fact that Christ now lives in you is even more unfathomable. "For in Christ all the fullness of the Deity lives in bodily form, and in Christ you have been brought to fullness" (Col. 2:9-10, NIV). The word *fullness* is the same in both instances. The fullness of God lived in Christ; the fullness of Christ lives in you as a new creation.

Butternut Squash Soup with Apricot Flavor Bomb

Coconut oil

1 each, butternut squash, large onion, large yam, diced

1 tsp salt, 1 pinch hot pepper powder, 2 TBS curry spices

One quart broth plus water

Flavor bomb, below

In the soup pot melt enough coconut oil to coat the bottom well. Fry the spices and pepper powder for a few seconds. Add the diced onion and salt. Stir, cook for 5 minutes or so letting onion weep. Add cubed squash and yam, broth and water to cover. Simmer until vegetables are soft. Cook enough so that you can process without the steam causing an eruption. If it's hot, you can add more water or cool broth to process it. Taste for salt and pepper.

Serve with Apricot flavor bomb: Coat the frying pan with coconut oil, add 1 tsp curry spice and ½ cup chopped walnuts. Stir fry for a minute. Add 1 TBS maple syrup and ½ cup chopped dried apricots.

If the only Bible passage I had access to was Colossians 1:15-27, that would be enough to make me happy the rest of my life! Here is the good news:

- Everything that exists, including you, was *in* Christ before the creation (v. 15-16).
- Everything that God is—His presence, power, and potential—dwelt bodily in Christ (v. 19).
- Everything that is Christ now lives in *you* (v. 27).
- Christ in *you* is the hope of glory (v. 27).

The word *glory* means reputation or substance. When you speak to someone on God's behalf or pray for them, you are releasing God's reputation and substance. When Paul says, "Christ in you is the hope of glory," he is stating, "God is in you and wants to get out!"

When God released created matter through His words, He was demonstrating the prophetic process. Creation was a prophetic process, and prophecy is co-laboring with God in a creative way to bring about His intentions on earth.

Habakkuk 2:14 (NIV) says, "For the earth will be filled with the knowledge of the glory of the Lord, as the waters cover the sea." If Christ in you is the hope of glory, then when Christ comes out of you, it will manifest His reputation and substance to the world. When you pray for someone in the bank, His glory covers that place. When you speak an encouraging word to a classmate, His glory covers your school.

We are surrounded by a raging world yearning for God. People are crying out for more, whether they understand what the more is or not. Their hope of glory is Christ in you. That glory can transform their lives.

God is in you and wants to get out. He's like a tiger in a too-tiny cage, yearning to get out and release the roar. He knows

He's the only hope for the world. You are His hands, feet, and mouth in the raging world.

CHAPTER 4

GOD'S SOUND PRODUCES SIGHT

"You can see God from anywhere if your mind is set to love and obey Him."

—A.W. Tozer, The Pursuit of God

"When we lift our inward eyes to gaze upon God we are sure to meet friendly eyes gazing back at us, for it is written that the eyes of the Lord run to and fro throughout all the earth. The sweet language of experience is "Thou God seest me." When the eyes of the soul looking out meet the eyes of God looking in, heaven has begun right here on this earth."

—A.W. Tozer

God's Sound Produces Sight

Wearing God Glasses

I like to do an exercise in my live events that demonstrates one way God can speak to us. In Jeremiah 1:11, God asked Jeremiah, "What do you see?" His simple answer was that he saw the branch of an almond tree. God's responded, "Yes! You have seen correctly. I am watching over my word." ("Watching over my word" was a play on words since the original word used for *watching* sounds almost identical to the word for *almond tree*.) God was showing Jeremiah that He could give him a spiritual message through an ordinary, natural object. God likes to put His super on our natural. I like to demonstrate that God speaks through ordinary objects by asking an event guest to hand me a personal possession, and I ask God to speak a spiritual message through it.

At one such event, I saw a young man sitting in the back row. I asked him if he would be willing to allow me to prophesy over him publicly using a simple object. He agreed, walked to the front, and handed me his sunglasses. I put them on and saw that they had a rose-colored tint, and immediately God started speaking to me about this man. The glasses reminded me of seeing through blood. "You have been looking at yourself through one set of lenses," I began, "but you are going to start seeing yourself through the blood of Jesus." This was the impression I felt God telling me because of the red tint on the lenses.

"People have said to you, 'You are just like this person,' but the problem is that person got into a lot of trouble. God doesn't look at you through those glasses. He looks at you through the rose-colored glasses of the blood of Jesus." I knew God had the man's attention at that point.

"Also, there's someone in your life who made wrong decisions that brought him into trouble with the law. You will go to people in prison, pray for them, and set them free. You are going to take these glasses to the person you care about in prison and put the glasses on him, and he will begin to see himself the way Jesus sees him."

I continued as I sensed God giving me more information. "I can also see that there was a dream in your heart that died. You wanted to be a hip-hop rapper. God says that you couldn't do it for the world, but you can do it for God. You will create a new sound of worship for a new generation. People wanted to give you a stage name, but God wants to give you the name 'son.' The old name people gave you was something that you would have hidden behind, but God is putting His name on you and taking the shame off your name."

By the time I finished the prophetic word, the young man was visibly touched and crying. After the service, I talked with him and learned that his parents were pastors, and he used to lead worship. He had fallen away from God and had attended the conference partly against his will. He told me about his friend in prison, and he also told me about his music career. He had signed a hip-hop contract and produced an album under a name that would not be appropriate to write in this book. The young man came back to God and eventually released an album under a new name. He visited his friend in prison, put the sunglasses on him, and told him what God sees in him. His friend gave his life to God. That young man still sings hip-hop and leads worship today.

God often has a different perspective than we do. He sees through correct lenses, and we need to learn how to see through

those lenses as well. This is important on two levels. First, like the young man at the conference, we need to see ourselves through the lens of our adoption as sons and daughters of God. Second, as we put on God glasses, we can see others as He sees them. We will never see ourselves correctly until we see God correctly. We can never see others correctly until we have a clear sight of God and ourselves.

Jesus showed us the way in Matthew 22:37-39 (NIV):

"Love the Lord your God with all your heart and with all your soul and with all your mind." This is the first and greatest commandment. And the second is like it: "Love your neighbor as yourself." All the Law and the Prophets hang on these two commandments.

Prophecy is motivated by the love of God. Paul told us to follow the way of love and eagerly desire spiritual gifts, especially prophecy (1 Cor. 14:1). Love is a key to prophecy. If you want to grow in the prophetic, grow in love. Jesus said all the prophets hang on this: love. You must first know and love God. Then, you can love yourself, which enables you to love your neighbor. You can only love your neighbor as you love yourself. A person who is self-critical is usually critical of others. When you realize how much God loves you, it is easy to love others!

A prophetic person who does not know God's love is scary. If I cannot believe God's best about me, how can I believe God's best about you? God has lenses of love. We have to learn to see through "God glasses."

God Saw the Light

Have you ever had the experience of not seeing something that was right in front of you? Like the missing keys that are in your hand or the lost sunglasses that are on your head? I have. Sometimes the obvious is not as clear to us as we think. At

times, our preconceptions can blind us from seeing clearly what is right in front of us. We may judge a person by first appearances or make assumptions about a situation without taking time to view it through God glasses.

Genesis 1:4 tells us that after God spoke the words, "Let there be light," He saw the light. When He saw it, He declared it was good. Prophecy is saying what God is saying. We cannot say what He says until we learn to see as He sees.

The word used when God *saw* the light is *ra'ah*. It means to discern, perceive, and envision. God didn't just passively observe the light; he discerned, perceived, and envisioned it. He saw *into* its purpose. He did not only look *at* the light, He looked *into* it.

When you understand the purpose of a something, you see it differently. If I opened the engine compartment to my car, I would look at it and see wires, metal stuff, and liquids. If an auto mechanic saw the same thing, he would be able to describe the purpose of each part and know how they fit and work together. That is *ra'ah,* to perceive purpose and discern with intention.

Ra'ah is used elsewhere in scripture to describe the ancient Hebrew prophets. They were called seers, the ones who could *ra'ah*.

Formerly in Israel, if someone went to inquire of God, they would say, "Come, let us go to the seer," because the prophet of today used to be called a seer.
~ 1 Samuel 9:9 (NIV)

God is demonstrating the prophetic process through the creative process. God was the first prophet, the first seer. Everything He created was designed for a purpose, and when He looks at His creation, He discerns, perceives, and envisions that purpose.

God sees us in the same way. He looks past the things we often see first: the mistakes, the clumsiness, or the shortcomings. He sees the destiny He placed within us from the moment of our creation. If we want to be good prophesiers, we must learn how to look through God glasses. We must refuse to merely see people; we must *ra'ah* people. When we prophesy, we must remember that discernment comes before description and seeing comes before saying. God calls everything that He creates good. When we see with God glasses, we will also see that it is good.

An online Future Coaching participant recently emailed me a testimony about how he was able to view someone through God glasses. He had been frustrated because someone had posted a very critical message on his Facebook page in response to his religious and political views. Feeling hurt by the exchange, the man wrote a polite reply to the lady and decided to stay off Facebook for a while.

Rather than remaining hurt and offended, the man asked God to give him a picture for her. In his mind's eye, he saw an image of a woman gently planting seeds in the ground. They were tree seeds. He also saw that the woman had already planted many of these seeds, and the trees were growing into a forest. She was instructing other women on how to plant trees. He asked God what this picture meant, and he sensed God telling him that this woman was gifted in teaching. She was called to mentor people. The man decided to send the lady another Facebook message, this time telling her the vision he had seen and the interpretation he felt God told him.

Despite their prior precarious interaction, the woman wrote back with a very different tone. She said that everything he described was true. It caused both the man and the woman to be able to see each other through God's eyes and set aside their differing opinions.

The man also told me in his email that God used the situation to change him. Now he understood better how to respond healthily to conflict. Rather than taking offense, he learned that he could ask God to show him how God views the other person. It changed his priorities. He realized that it is not important that people agree with him on the hot topics of religion or politics. Rather, the importance lies in the value of the people themselves and seeing them as God sees them.

Who You Are and Who You Aren't

After God saw the light, Genesis 1:4 (NIV) says, "He separated the light from the darkness." The word *separate* means to distinguish from or differentiate. When God sees the purpose of the light, He also recognizes what it is not. It is not darkness.

 @bob_hazlett

Speaking the truth in love does not mean telling someone what you think about them. It means telling what God thinks about them.

Part of the prophetic process is discerning what or whom people are not. God separated the light for its intended purpose and away from what was not its purpose. I believe prophecy sets people into their purpose and away from that which is not their purpose. There is a corrective element there, but it is positive correction, not negative correction. Prophetic ministry should point people to who they are. When that happens, issues of sins and spiritual bondage will naturally be confronted, sometimes unknowingly.

One night I was in a meeting and as I was teaching, I approached a row of seats where I saw a young lady with close-cropped hair seated with a group of people. As I approached her, I noticed that she avoided eye contact. Initially, I thought she was feeling intimidated. Sometimes people think prophetic ministers see all their sin and want to expose it. To put her at ease, I started by saying, "You don't have to be afraid of me. I only have good news for you." I began to tell her that God was going to use her to be a person of prayer and worship and through her singing people would find God and be set free from spiritual bondages.

Her face became hardened and she folded her arms. I could see something was keeping her from receiving these words. I quietly asked God to show me what was blocking her. Immediately, I saw a picture of her as an eight-year-old girl. I saw very bad things that happened to her at the hands of men who were supposed to have protected her. I simultaneously knew that she had experienced physical and sexual abuse and as a result had turned away from relationships with men and had many unhealthy relationships with women.

It would have been inappropriate for me to share these things publicly, so I said, "The person you became at eight years old is not the person you were created to be. God is fixing what was broken when you were eight." The scene that followed was not what I expected. The forces that had kept her true identity captive immediately rose up inside of her. She screamed out loudly and her body began to convulse. I knew that this was a demonic force I was dealing with. A lying voice had humiliated her in private for much of her life, and I did not want to see her humiliated publicly, so I muted my microphone. I quietly spoke into her ear. I told every spiritual force that had kept her bound from age eight that it was time to go.

She immediately calmed down and I asked her to stand up. I finished sharing the words I had begun before I was interrupted. I told her all that God was going to use her to do. She was visibly emotional, so I asked for some spiritual mothers to come forward, hold her, and assure her of God's love.

Several years later, a young lady approached me at a different meeting in the same city. "Do you remember me?" she asked. It was the same young lady, though I did not immediately recognize her. She had grown her hair out, and her face was glowing. She told me her life was changed, and she was leaving for a ministry school where she would be studying worship and prayer. When God tells you who you are, who you are not has to go!

Prophecy is positive correction. Negative correction comes from a critical perspective. It seeks to expose the problem. Positive correction seeks to expose the potential. When God spoke, He called the light day. He did not say, "You are not night." I believe there is a corrective element to prophecy, but it is for a redemptive purpose.

When God tells us who we are, we will be able to identify who we are not. Prophetic words do the same for us. Sometimes we see ourselves wrongly; we don't see through God glasses for ourselves. When we hear God's roar correctly identifying who He has called us to be, we are able to distinguish between our self-image and God's image in us. We become empowered to stop trying to be who we are not.

I learned the power of this principle again not long ago. I was speaking to a couple about their future. I knew the man was a police officer, but I told him that God was making him a spiritual S.W.A.T. (special forces) officer. I saw him passing up a promotion in order to put his family first, and another promotion was coming that would be even better. God saw him as a good officer, but more importantly, God saw him as a great dad.

This word greatly touched the man and his wife. He had just been offered a promotion to become a S.W.A.T. officer, but because it would take him away from his family, he was

conflicted about the decision. Because of the prophetic word, he realized it was more important to be a dad and husband than to take the promotion.

That prophetic word empowered the man to choose to be whom God had called him to be—a great dad. It also empowered him to choose to not be who he wasn't called to be—a S.W.A.T. officer. The statement that God saw him as a great dad gave him the courage to walk away from a promotion that would separate him from his true identity. It was a defining word for that moment of his life.

A similar circumstance occurred in the Bible with Jacob. He had spent his entire life cheating and conniving to get his way. Genesis 32 describes how he spent a night wrestling with God and insisted on God's blessing before he entered the next season of his life. Not only did God bless him, but He gave him a new name. He changed his name from Jacob, which meant "deceiver," to Israel, which meant "he strives with God." No longer was he to be known by deception and trickery. His life would now be defined by the blessing he received when he strove with God. This one simple word spoken from God redefined the course of his life. He became the father of the nation of Israel and the foundation for God's chosen people.

Hebrews 4:12 (NIV) tells us,

For the word of God is alive and active. Sharper than any double-edged sword, it penetrates even to dividing soul and spirit, joints and marrow; it judges the thoughts and attitudes of the heart.

Whether they are spoken to us or through us, God's prophetic words separate. They distinguish light from darkness, and they penetrate down to the human spirit. A person's greatest potential resides deep down in their spirit where God's divine nature dwells, but most of their problems reside in their physical bodies or emotions and thoughts of the soul. God's word can address all three.

The greatest transformation takes place when God's word reaches down through the problems of the body or soul and awakens a dead spirit to life. He deposits a seed of destiny in a spirit that was dormant, and it cuts through all the challenges of the body and soul. The word circumvents the problems and pulls out the potential. In the process, the original problem can be confronted or eliminated. Many times physical and emotional healing happens when this occurs. I call this turning a person inside out through prophecy.

I first observed this phenomenon when I was speaking with a teenage girl. I shared a prophetic impression that God wanted to use her to be a worshipper who leads people into God's presence. She petulantly rolled her eyes at me like many teenagers do at their parents. I wasn't sure what to do.

Setting my own judgments aside, I looked at her again through God glasses, and another picture developed. I saw her standing in front of her mirror in her bedroom singing into her hairbrush. I was surprised when she cracked a reluctant smile at me. I knew I had her then! I told her I heard her singing a specific song from a specific singer, and it wasn't a worship song. When I started singing it, she started laughing. I told her she wanted to be just like that person, but someone had told her she couldn't sing well. Now she only sang in her room. At those words, she started to get emotional.

I told her that her heavenly Father loves to hear her sing that song. We were both weeping, and the tears were bringing healing to her fractured soul. That is when I reached down into her spirit and spoke the words of destiny that I had tried unsuccessfully to speak at the beginning. This time, she was able

to receive it. God had called her to be a worshipper who leads people into God's presence.

God's word is sharp and precise. It can speak to physical circumstances, emotional states, and cut down to the spirit to plant seeds of life. When I reach down into a person's spirit and pull out their potential, the problems in their bodies and soul are often removed.

Seeing in the Right Order

If I were to have seen that young lady in a different order, the outcome would not have been good. I could have seen her first according to the flesh—with the rolled eyes and scowled face—and thought there was no hope for her. Instead, I changed the order in which I saw. I looked to God first. I acknowledged His goodness, His love for the girl, and His desire to bring her destiny into reality. Then I was able to see the girl as God sees her. Sometimes we see wrongly because we don't see in the right order.

Prior to the fall of Adam and Eve into sin, they saw with God glasses. After their sin, something shifted. For the first time, they noticed they were naked. They started seeing primarily according to the flesh. Something they had been unaware of before now became a very big problem for them. We also are too keenly skilled at seeing ourselves and others only according to the flesh. We make judgments based on what we see of peoples' behaviors, choices, attitudes, and actions. However, this is not how God sees. He sees according to His destiny on a person.

I want to see as God sees. In order to do so, I must first see God rightly. I come to know Him better in two ways: through the Word of God and through relationship with the Holy Spirit. As I know God more intimately, I know better how He sees His children.

Second, as I behold God and focus my attention on who He is, I am better able to see myself clearly. I realize that I am an adopted son who is cherished and called to an amazing destiny because I am a child of the King. When I see myself in that light, I am not afraid to walk in the purpose God has called me to. I stop focusing on myself and trying to find significance. I learn to rest in the fact that my significance comes from His love for me. It frees me to just be God's son and not strive to be accepted by Him. When we know what God says about us, we can rest in that knowledge. When you are doing what God has called you to do, it's not work; it's rest. If you are not in rest, you are in stress.

 @bob_hazlett

Jesus said critical words destroy the image of God in man. That's murder. Likewise, self-critical words destroy God's plan in you.

Third, after we see God correctly and see ourselves correctly, we can begin to see others the way God sees them— through the lens of His love for them. We refuse to follow Adam and Eve's example to see according to the flesh, and we begin to see through the eyes of the Spirit. It may not seem like this will come easily, but God is quick to give grace. He desires to speak to and through you, and He empowers you to do it every step of the way.

CHAPTER 5

GOD'S SOUND EXPANDS THE ENVIRONMENT

*"Yet if we would know God and for other's sake tell
what we know we must try to speak of his love. All
Christians have tried but none has ever done it very well.
I can no more do justice to that awesome and
wonder-filled theme than a child can grasp a star. Still by
reaching toward the star the child may call attention to it
and even indicate the direction one must look to see it.
So as I stretch my heart toward the high shining love of
God someone who has not before known about it may
be encouraged to look up and have hope."*

—A.W. Tozer, The Knowledge of the Holy

God's Sound Expands the Environment

Spiritual Frames

When I was dating my wife in college, I dreamed about our future together. One roadblock was clear to me: In order to have a future with my wife in it, her father would have to envision a future with me in it. He was visiting the college campus one day when I asked how he was doing. He said, "I am busier than a one-armed paper hanger." He was hanging a wallpaper mural in my wife's small dorm room, and he felt he could use another hand. It was the perfect opportunity to insert myself into the picture. We finished the job together, and the landscape mural covering the whole wall made the tiny dorm room look surprisingly bigger. That picture without a frame created the appearance of open space and a roomy environment. My offer to help hang it created space for me too!

Thoughts and ideas create pictures, and words frame those ideas. God's words framed the world. Hebrews 11:3 (NKJV) says,

> *By faith we understand that the worlds were framed by the word of God, so that the things which are seen were not made of things which are visible.*

The pictures we create become the words we speak and, many times, the future we live. Out of a man's heart, he speaks; what he thinks about himself in his heart he becomes (Luke 6:45, Prov. 23:7). If you want to change the future you need a new picture. However, without the right frame, the picture will not fit. Seeing what God sees forms the picture; saying what God says creates the frame. A natural frame creates a border or limit for a picture. Prophecy is a spiritual frame that does the opposite: it expands the borders and erases the limits of the future.

Genesis 1:7-8 (NIV) tells us,

So God made the vault and separated the water under the vault from the water above it. And it was so. God called the vault "sky."

The word *vault* means a visible arch. When God put a frame around the world it was an expansive, visible environment that appeared limitless. God's sound created a frame into which all visible creation would be placed. I believe this is a picture of how prophecy gives us vision, opens us up to new possibilities, and expands our perspective of the future.

Jeremiah seemed to be limited by his environment. God gave him a job, and he tried to quit before he even started. God's response to Jeremiah's every objection was truth. When Jeremiah stated that he was only a child, God replied with, "I saw you before that." When Jeremiah added that he was not a good speaker, God declared, "I am with you!"

Jeremiah had the same problem many of us have. Our biggest challenge is not the task God put before us but who we believe we are. Prophecy has the ability to erase the limited frames that culture or experience places on us and reframes our future with God's words. God sees you in your future today! Prophecy removes the limitation that an earthly identity and perspective enforces on you. Your greatest limitation doesn't lie in your credentials or experience; it lies between your ears in your thinking!

 @bob_hazlett

When you know more about what God thinks about you, you will usually respond less to what others think.

God had called Jeremiah to prophesy to nations. Jeremiah never held a passport or flew in an airplane. He didn't possess diplomatic status or linguistic skills. In fact, he never left his hometown. But he changed the world! Prophetic people see big opportunities in small places. They expect big impact from small acts. When God touched Jeremiah's mouth, everything changed (Jer. 1:9-10). God's words reframed Jeremiah's future so he could see without limits.

Big Presents in Small Packages

On the third day of creation, God said, "Let the land produce vegetation: seed-bearing plants and trees on the land that bear fruit with seed in it" (Gen. 1:11, NIV). The first thing God created that had the power to reproduce was seed-bearing plants. Everything big starts with something small. This is true in nature as well as spirituality. It is especially true when it comes to prophecy.

When God wanted to change human history, He sent the Word (Jesus). Jesus was not called the story, book, or sentence; He was called the Word. His appearance as a baby born in a manger is a testimony to this truth. Small words still cause huge impact. Matthew 13:31-32 (NKJV) admonishes us,

> *The kingdom of heaven is like a mustard seed, which a man took and sowed in his field, which indeed is the least of all the seeds; but when it is grown it is greater than the herbs and becomes a tree, so that the birds of the air come and nest in its branches.*

Don't underestimate the power of a small encouragement or a seemingly insignificant prophetic utterance. God still uses words as seeds to bring great harvest.

I fly in airplanes a lot, so it's not unusual for me engage in a conversation with another passenger that leads to sharing a spiritual impression. I was sitting next to a young woman on one such occasion when I felt impressed that God wanted me to tell her that with God an accident can turn into something good. This seemed like a small word to me, and I asked God for more detail before I shared it with the woman. I then had a strong impression that she had a dog. I asked God to tell me the name of her pet, thinking this would get her attention. My request was met by silence.

I have since learned when God gives you a little bit at first it is because He has much more in store for you, like the mustard seed. He wants you to be faithful with the little so He can give you much. I decided to share what little I had. When I did, her eyes swelled with tears as she told me she had just been released from the hospital that morning. She had been in a car accident three days before, and it was a miracle she survived.

This small word turned into an encounter that changed her life. I prayed for her body, and all the effects of her accident were completely healed! That would have been enough, but God had also showed me that she was returning home to her parents and that she was going to tell them she was pregnant. She asked how I knew this. I told her, "God is a master at taking accidents and making something good out of them." We agreed together in prayer, and she gave her life to Christ. What I saw as small was a big deal to God!

Big presents often come in small packages. We see this truth when we look at the last twelve prophetic voices in the Old Covenant. These books are commonly called the Minor Prophets. Their combined message could be summarized in one sentence: God is a big God with a big family and big plans. God's people may think small, but God does not. The length of the minor prophets' words is but a whisper compared to the rest of the Bible; however, their voices continue to reverberate. The

prophetic gift today still has the ability to take a small word and make a big impact!

Prophecy puts God back at the center and offers people a bigger picture for their lives—God's picture. When we hear God's plan for our lives, it is humbling. Prophecy tells people that God thinks they are important enough to stop the world for them.

I was recently teaching in another country in a large conference setting. As I taught, I was unaware that a woman in the room was thinking to herself, *I wish God would tell him to speak something to me.* A voice spoke back to her: "You are not important enough. He would never speak to you." She got discouraged and quietly left.

As I continued teaching, I felt that in order to demonstrate the point I was making, we needed to separate the crowd into groups of two. They would then ask God to speak something to their partner. It took several minutes with the help of the interpreter to pair everyone. I asked if there was anyone left who did not find a partner. The woman who had left returned because she had forgotten something at her seat. I saw her walking alone and called from the front, "Do you have a partner?" She looked confused, so I said, "Come to the front. You will be my partner. God has something to say to you."

She fell to the floor in tears before she even made it to the front. God had already spoken to her. "You are important enough for me."

The prophet Joel, a minor prophet, had some big words for the Church. His prophecy became the birthday message that Peter preached on the Day of Pentecost.

"I will pour out my Spirit on all people. Your sons and daughters will prophesy, your old men will dream

dreams, your young men will see visions. Even on my servants, both men and women, I will pour out my Spirit in those days. I will show wonders in the heavens and on the earth."

~ Joel 2:28-30 (NIV)

Prophecy reveals that there is no one too small for God to put His Spirit inside. In 1999, I was beginning to learn about prophecy. In the first meeting I had that year, God told me to pray and prophesy only over children ages ten and under. I prayed for about seventy children that first meeting, and I continued to do that in every meeting. After three months, I had prayed for hundreds of children. Finally, I asked God why He wanted me to only pray for kids. "I want you to use simple words that are easy to understand," He explained. "If a child can understand you, anyone can understand you."

Since then, I have prophesied to many types of people: businesspeople and government officials, people in the church and outside the church, the famous and the unknown. It is the job of prophetic people to make God accessible to others. That requires us to simplify hearing God and understanding His voice.

God's Sound Changes Times and Seasons

I was surprised to discover I have two birthdays. I am not referring to a natural birthday and a spiritual birthday. I have two birth certificates with two different dates on them. I noticed this while gathering information for my college admissions application and looking through some school paperwork my parents had saved. I found a handwritten birth certificate with the date September 29 signed by the doctor. That was strange to me since my birthday is September 28, as noted on the type-written hospital birth certificate.

"I have two birthdays!" I told my mother. I was hoping to collect on past birthday presents owed me. My mother explained to me that I was born on the day that clocks were turned back one hour at midnight. Since I was born a few minutes after that on September 29, I was actually born on September 28. I got in one day early!

That is a parable for my life. It is also one of the characteristics of prophecy. Prophecy has the ability to look into the past, present, and future and interpret them from God's perspective. Prophecy also partners with God to make up for lost time or reverse the effects of negative past events. Daniel stated it this way: "He [God] changes the times and the seasons" (Dan. 2:21, NIV). Daniel was able to prophetically interpret what God was doing within the context of time and to accelerate God's people into a season of destiny.

Times and seasons are not something you will find in heaven. They are part of the visible creation. Genesis 1:14 (NKJV) tells us,

> *Then God said, "Let there be lights in the firmament of the heavens to divide the day from the night; and let them be for signs and seasons, and for days and years."*

When God created light, He designated a portion of it to be time specific: day. There was no day until God created it. Seasons came into being when God created the cosmos. He put the sun, moon, and stars in the sky for signs and seasons. These things govern the earth but not heaven. God exists outside the governing sphere of earth; He rules in heaven, which is outside the constraints of time and seasons.

Under the Old Covenant, Isaiah 49 tells us God answers in the "time of His favor" and He helps in the "day of salvation." Under the New Covenant, the apostle Paul defined when that time and day occurred: *now* is the time of favor and *today* is the day of salvation (2 Cor. 6:2). Jesus said it another way: a time is coming and *now* is (John 4:23, 5:25). God does not exist in time; He exists in eternal now. The time in heaven is now, and the date in heaven is today.

Ezekiel had a vision of heaven. He saw a throne and a river coming from it. In Revelation, the apostle John confirmed that vision. Alongside the river were trees that bore fruit continually. They had fruit at different levels of maturity at all time. Their leaves, which never withered, were for the healing of the nations. The only season in heaven is fruit-growing and fruit-yielding season. Psalm 1 declares that righteous people are like those trees—their leaves never wither, and they bear fruit every season.

Prophecy helps to get us connected with the time and the season of heaven for the birthing, maturing, and yielding of fruit in our lives. Prophecy makes up for lost time.

Delays and Dreams

Prophetic promises don't always come to fulfillment quickly. God exists outside time, though He intercepts time constantly to speak with us and interject His destiny into our lives. We must be cautious not to allow our hearts to become cold when our dreams are delayed. There are four keys I have learned when dealing with delays: thanksgiving, rejoicing with those who rejoice, prayer and worship, and persistence.

 @bob_hazlett

Sometimes, the right thing to say when you are going through a struggle is nothing. Better yet, find out what God says and say that!

Several years ago I was feeling stuck waiting for God's promises in my life. I found myself asking God for wisdom about how to get things moving when I came across this scripture:

*Be anxious for nothing, but in everything by prayer and supplication, **with thanksgiving, let your requests be made known to God.***
~ Philippians 4:6 (NKJV; emphasis added)

After meditating on that scripture, I had an idea to have a Thanksgiving dinner with my family. I decided we would do it in April. (In America, we celebrate Thanksgiving in November to remember God's provision for the founders of our nation.) I decided we would thank God for the provision that was yet to come. I told my family the plan to make a complete Thanksgiving dinner and take time to thank God for all He had done for us while also bringing our requests in prayer to Him. When I explained my plan to my wife and children, my ten-year-old daughter said, "Dad, that is so weird that we are doing this." I tried to stop her to explain the spiritual significance, but she continued, "Just today, I was on the computer, and as a joke, I emailed a Thanksgiving Day card to you and mom." God had aligned my whole family to the new season already! Giving thanks aligns us to a new season.

When you are in a delayed season, you have the option to either rejoice or complain. Sometimes that choice is made even harder when you see others receive an answer you have been waiting for. A second key to dealing with delays to your promises is to rejoice with those who rejoice. In 2008, God spoke to me, "This year, you will prophesy things to people that you have been waiting for a long time in your life, and you will see it come to pass quickly for them." He wanted to teach me how to rejoice with those who rejoice, even when I was in a season of delayed dreams.

I remember prophesying to a pastor one Sunday morning, "God is going to bless you with a home. You are not even looking for one, but your wife has been, and she has great faith. Get packing! God is going to do this quickly." I cringed on the inside, because I knew I really wanted a new home as well. I had to choose to be thankful and rejoice with this man.

The pastor called me the next day saying he had been unaware that his wife had been looking at houses. He received a phone call on Sunday afternoon from someone in his church who was on an airplane on Sunday morning. Right about the time I was prophesying, his plane was reaching cruising altitude and he heard the pilot say, "We have reached 30,000 feet." The man instead heard God say, "Give your pastor $30,000." I had been praying for a home for ten years, and in less than ten hours after my prophecy, this pastor was on his way to home ownership. I was truly happy for him, but I had to *choose* to rejoice. I did that many times that year!

If you have read the book of Daniel, you will know that it contains a lot of dreams and dream interpretation. Most of those dreams concerned times and seasons that were coming in the future. Many of them were sealed up until the end of days. Daniel and his people were living in a delay. A Babylonian king named Nebuchadnezzar had conquered them. Jeremiah had prophesied that they would be in captivity for seventy years. Daniel found this prophecy and began to petition God about it. Daniel, respected by the king and empire leaders alike, had enjoyed great favor in this new land. However, in Daniel 2 his life was threatened if he could not interpret the king's dream. Great wisdom was necessary for him to save his life and the lives of the other righteous men. When he received divine interpretation of the king's dream, Daniel declared,

> *To You, O God of my fathers, I give thanks and praise,*
> *For You have given me wisdom and power; Even now*
> *You have made known to me what we requested of You,*
> *For You have made known to us the king's matter.*
> *~ Daniel 2:23 (NASB)*

Daniel had to be the source of giving meaning to someone else's dream even as his dream was being delayed and he was threatened with death. Daniel personified what is admonished in Proverbs 11:25: When we refresh others, we will also be refreshed. Learn to rejoice when others rejoice!

Daniel discovered a third key during times of delayed dreams: prayer and worship. As soon as Daniel started to pray for the fulfillment of God's promises, the enemy did not like it. If he could not get Daniel to complain, he would stop Daniel from praying. The king passed a law that no one could pray, including Daniel who was praying for the return of his people to rebuild the temple as was prophesied by Jeremiah. This was Daniel's response to the ban:

> *Now when Daniel knew that the document was signed,*
> *he entered his house (now in his roof chamber he had*
> *windows open toward Jerusalem); and he continued*
> *kneeling on his knees three times a day, praying.*
> *~ Daniel 6:10 (NASB)*

Daniel committed himself to prayer. Daniel's open window toward Jerusalem was a prophetic picture. Worship keeps the windows open and your eyes focused toward your promise. When you are in a delay, sometimes the last thing you want to do is worship or pray. There was a time when I did not want to go to any meetings because I was a magnet for prophecies, and I did not want any more. Rather, I wanted the prophecies I had already received to come to pass. I was stuck in dream delay. Despite my best efforts to hide in the back of the church behind a plastic tree, I would still get called out for a prophecy. More than once, the prophecy was, "You are in a delay, but God is going to speed things up." I did not want to hear that; I wanted to see it happen!

The delays ended when I decided that God would not give up on my promises so I would not either. I reflected on all my recorded promises, composed them into songs, and sang them back to God. I spent many mornings with my guitar alone with God, worshipping and singing my prophecies. The reason He was giving me words about time accelerating was that He had not forgotten my promises, and He did not want me to forget them either. Like Daniel, we all need to learn how to open the window, look into our promises, and worship.

Daniel also learned a fourth key during seasons of delayed promises: persistence. He was an old man when he wrote this:

> *I, Daniel, observed in the books the number of the years which was revealed as the word of the Lord to Jeremiah the prophet for the completion of the desolations of Jerusalem, namely, seventy years. So I gave my attention to the Lord God to seek Him by prayer and supplications, with fasting, sackcloth and ashes.*
> *~ Daniel 9:2-3 (NASB)*

Daniel kept his heart, his body, and his gift pure before God and man. He served four different kings. He survived an assassination attempt, an entrapment scheme, and a lion's den. Even after all that, he was focused on God's desires for his nation. His dream was bigger than just him. When you press through the delays and damaging circumstances, you realize that your dream is bigger than you are. When that happens God is willing to fight for you. If your dream is little, you will have a little fight and need little resources for its fulfillment. When your dream is bigger than you, bigger than your family, big enough for a nation, then God will bring big resources. There may be a big delay, but God has a bigger answer. After much delay, Daniel's big answer came in the form of an angel:

> *Do not be afraid, Daniel. Since the first day that you set your mind to gain understanding and to humble yourself before your God, your words were heard, and I have*

*come in response to them. **But** the prince of the Persian kingdom resisted me twenty-one days.*
~ Daniel 10:12-13 (NIV; emphasis added)

There was something big causing the delay. God sent Daniel's answer the first day he humbled himself. If you are humbly waiting on the fulfillment of God's promises to you, God has already sent them. But something is delaying it. In front of your future season, there is a big *but*. It is common for me to hear people say, "God told He would do this, *but . . .*" or "His Word speaks truth, *but . . .*" There is always a *but* in the way of your answer. The good news is God is going to release a *big* angel to kick that *big but* out of the way! Like Daniel, persistence is a key for us when we face all those *buts*.

 @bob_hazlett

The best dreams left untried remain only good ideas. If never attempted, they are never achieved.

Do not give up your attitude of gratitude. Do not become weary in well doing. Do not forget His promises. Do not let anything steal your worship. Open your window and look at your promise. God's words not only set times and seasons, they change times and seasons. Prophecy gets you caught up to the season you should be in and makes up for lost time you experienced in the past.

Signs of the Times

I believe a miracle occurs when we become aware of what God has already done and access it by faith. The miracle of new birth happens when people become aware of the death and resurrection of Jesus. When they believe with their hearts and confess with their mouths, what Jesus did two thousand years ago becomes reality in their present lives. Today is the day of salvation. When we pray for the sick and see them recover, we take hold of, by faith, what Jesus did for them. Our prayer accesses the finished work of the cross. In the same way, I believe prophecy allows us to access what God has already said about a person and what He intends for them. According to Paul in Ephesians 2:10 (NIV), they "are God's handiwork, created in Christ Jesus to do good works, which God prepared in advance for [them] to do." Just as a road sign points to a destination, prophecy points to who they are and what they are created to do. Signs are one of God's sounds.

I hate to admit it, but the first time I took my driving test I failed. I scored 100 percent on the written exam. My vision was a perfect 20/20. I even nailed the dreaded parallel parking portion—not an easy task in my mom's 1976 AMC Pacer. Google it. It was voted the worst car of all time! I did not fail because I had an ugly car. I failed for one simple reason: I neglected to heed a sign—the stop sign—for the required three seconds. I saw the sign. I intended to obey it. I even stopped for a split second, but that was not enough. I needed to follow through with what the sign required. Believe me, the next time I took the test, I watched for that sign, and I came to a full stop. If I had to wait until grass started to grow through the pavement under my tires, I was not going to fail a second time!

Signs are important. They require attention and intention. But they also require bold action. That is why they are called signs. They point you in the direction you need to go and act.

God often places signs around us throughout our daily lives. Sometimes they are so seemingly mundane that we miss them. When my wife notices the birthdate of one of our children as a time on a digital clock, she uses it as a sign that they need attention at that moment. They get a lot of text messages from her when the clock says 4:14 or 6:26. Their birth dates act as signs.

Moses was a man whose birth and life was filled with signs. He was rescued from the water, and that is what his name means. His deliverance and his name became a sign for the nation of Israel, which later would be rescued and pass through the Red Sea to their deliverance. His birth and life became a vivid picture of the birth of a nation. Usually, the more deliberate the sign, the more difficult it will be to the reach destination.

God gave Moses a difficult task, but He also gave him a powerful tool to carry it out. "Take this staff in your hand so you can perform the signs with it" (Ex. 4:17, NIV). When you have lived in slavery for over 400 years, it difficult to see a way out. You need a sign to point the way. In Moses' case, God gave him more than one: ten to be exact! Each plague was a sign that pointed to one of the Egyptian gods that was a roadblock to Israel's journey to freedom.

Sign	Roadblock
Nile water into blood	Hapi (god of the Nile)
Frogs	Hekhet (goddess of fertility, frog-headed)
Gnats or lice from dust	Geb (god of the earth)
Flies (gadflies)	Khepri (god of resurrection, beetle-headed)
Cattle/livestock disease	Hathor (goddess of protection, cow-headed)
Boils	Isis (goddess of medicine and peace)
Thunder/hail	Nut (goddess of the sky)
Locusts	Senehem (god of protection from ravages of pests, locust-headed)
Darkness	Ra or Amon-Ra (god of the sun)
Death of the firstborn	Pharaoh himself (he and his firstborn were gods)[v]

You Have to See a Sign to Believe It

Jesus said in Matt 16:4 (NKJV), "A wicked and adulterous generation seeks after a sign, and no sign shall be given to it." That is strong language, but a little further study will reveal that the word *wicked* has two meanings. Spiritually speaking, it means evil; physically speaking, it means diseased or blinded. I am not sure why an evil person would look for a sign, but I do know why a blinded person needs one. They need to see!

Jesus also uses the word *adulterous*. Jesus defines adultery as not only physical; it is visual and emotional as well (Matt. 5:28). The leaders Jesus was speaking to were in love with an idea of God's kingdom that was not God's intention. They had to see it, feel it, and touch it to know it had really come. They had been ruled with religious oppression for so long that power had become their mistress. That is why they had a love/hate affair with Jesus' power. One of their leaders summed it up: "Rabbi, we know that you are a teacher who has come from God. For no one could perform the signs you are doing if God were not with him" (John 3:2, NIV). Jesus' response to all the demands for signs was, "If you believed Moses, you would believe me; for he wrote about me" (John 5:46, NIV). Moses was a sign that pointed to Jesus.

 @bob_hazlett

Whatever God calls you to do, He also empowers you to do.
Especially if it is impossible!

Signs are especially helpful when we are walking through a season blindly. God may use a sign to guide us through situations we might miss and point us to part of our destiny that may be unknown to us. Some of these are small moments when circumstances are symbolic and life becomes a lesson. Signs are a regular part of my communication with God. I don't ask for them; they just happen. God does not want me to be blind. He wants me to see.

One day several years ago, God spoke to me as I read this passage of scripture:

> *What I am saying is that as long as an heir is underage,*
> *he is no different from a slave, although he owns the*

*whole estate. The heir is subject to guardians and trustees until the time set by his father. So also, when we were underage, we were in slavery under the elemental spiritual forces of the world. **But when the set time had fully come, God sent his Son.***

~ Galatians 4:1-4 (NIV; emphasis added)

I heard God say to me, "You are living behind your time." I asked God what that meant. He showed me that He had made me a son, given me the whole estate, but I was living like a guest in the guest room. I was waiting for an upgrade that I had already been given. He said it was already the fullness of time, He was sending me as His son, and He would give me a sign to point me to it. He said, "In the next week you will see the number 44 many times and it will remind you to live in the fullness of time." I understood from this that 44 was a reminder to me of Galatians 4:4.

That weekend, I was traveling to a conference by airplane. I sat down in my seat and double-checked my boarding pass to make sure I was seated correctly. That is when I noticed that I was on flight 44 and in row 44. That may have been a coincidence, but I tucked it away in the back of my mind. My driver picked me up, and as we exited the highway for the hotel, I noticed the exit number was 44. When we arrived at the hotel, my driver went inside to check me into my room while I waited in the car. I glanced at the clock that read 4:44. I have heard it said, "God's signs can make you wonder." God had already told me what these signs meant.

I had two hours to rest before the night meeting, but my rest was interrupted with a call from the front desk telling me I had a visitor. I went downstairs to find a minister who I had met the previous year. He lived an hour away but traveled to give me a message. That morning, he had a vision of me as he was praying for me. "God is putting a gun in your hand," he said. "It is a Magnum .44." I knew immediately what this meant. Not only was I living in my fullness of time, but also God was giving me a spiritual weapon— prophecy—that would shoot people into their future!

We know God is always with us. That is the definition of faith, knowing God is here even if it looks and feels like He is not. However, I love when God makes His presence known. Signs are one of the ways God lets us see Him, feel Him, and touch Him.

Many signs accompanied Jesus' life: a star at His birth, a dove at His baptism, an earthquake at His death, and a cloud at His resurrection. Signs are one of God's love languages. They could be in the form of a number on a clock, a sign on the road, or even a symbolic vision. God's sound speaks in signs.

God's voice created the environment and atmosphere for man to live in relationship with the Creator and the creation. Prophecy creates an atmosphere for people to fulfill their vertical purpose of relationship with God and their horizontal purpose of relationship with creation. Psalm 19:1 (NIV) says, "The heavens declare the glory of God; the skies proclaim the work of his hands." Signs are all around us. The created world is the canvas upon which God crafts His signs. His words spoken into the void of your life rumble and disrupt every obstacle between you and your God-ordained purpose. When the raging world tries to put boundaries and barriers on your destiny, the heavens roar, "The sky is the limit!"

CHAPTER 6
GOD'S SOUND SPEAKS

"Between the scribe who has read and the prophet who has seen there is a difference as wide as the sea. We are today overrun with orthodox scribes, but the prophets, where are they? The hard voice of the scribe sounds over evangelicalism, but the Church waits for the tender voice of the saint who has penetrated the veil and has gazed with inward eye upon the Wonder that is God. And yet, thus to penetrate, to push in sensitive living experience into the holy Presence, is a privilege open to every child of God."

—A.W. Tozer, The Pursuit of God

God's Sound Speaks

The Roar Whispers

The word *roar* in English connotes a booming, rumbling voice, and it is often associated with fear. As I studied the Hebrew word *qol* (Strong's 6963), I came to realize that the same word has a different connotation in the original language. *Qol* does mean a loud, vociferous roar, but it can also be translated as voice, noise, sound, thunder, and even whisper. Moreover, in the Hebrew mind, everything God created has its own voice, its own *qol.*

The famous medieval Jewish scholar Moses Maimonides explains that all created objects, even the celestial bodies, are "endowed with life and serve their Lord . . . He [the psalmist in Psalm 19] describes the heavens themselves as in reality praising God and declaring His wonders."[vi] All creation hears, responds to, and joins in the roar.

Elijah experienced this in 1 Kings 19:11-13 (NIV):

> *Then a great and powerful wind tore the mountains apart and shattered the rocks before the Lord, but the Lord was not in the wind. After the wind there was an earthquake, but the Lord was not in the earthquake. After the earthquake came a fire, but the Lord was not in the fire. And after the fire came a gentle whisper* [qol]. *Elijah heard it.*

When Elijah was struggling to hear God's voice, he heard many sounds. In that moment, God's voice was not wind, the earthquake, or the fire. His sound was in the whisper—a still, small voice. Proximity and position are the two factors that determine the tone and volume you use when speaking to someone. When you are close to them, you do not have to shout. Likewise, when you have relationship and influence with someone, you rarely have to raise your voice to be heard. I love when God speaks in dramatic form and fashion. However, I believe He desires to be so close to us that all we need is a whisper to hear Him. God came very close to man in order to breathe life into Him. God's breath stamped the image of God onto man and deposited the sound of God into man.

God's Stamp

Last year, I received an iPad as a gift. At the time, they were running a promotion for two free lines of engraving on the back. Since my name only required one line, I thought I would engrave a distinctive identification on the second. It reads,

Bob Hazlett
Son of God

Recently, I had reason to be very glad I had stamped that engraving on the iPad. I had left it on an airplane, and the person who found it turned it in promptly. I'm not sure if the motivation was honesty or fear. Who would want to mess with God's son? The moniker sounds kind of funny, but it's accurate. My earthly name is Bob, but my heavenly name is son. I've been stamped!

God did the same thing eons ago at creation. "God called the light 'day'" (Gen. 1:5, NIV). Everything He created, He put His stamp on. When you stamp something, you assign ownership to it. Just as the stamp on my iPad identified it as my possession, so also God has placed His stamp on every individual. When you stamp something, you also define its purpose and function. Before God stamped the light, it was just light. After He stamped it, it was day.

Prophecy identifies God's stamp on a person's life. It assigns possession to God and defines the person's purpose. It calls a person by the name God gave them.

Today, we use names as identifiers for people, places, and things. However, in ancient Hebrew culture, a name had symbolic and prophetic significance. In fact, the name of a person identified directly with that person's life, reputation, character, and spiritual destiny. When God called the light day, He identified its reputation, character, and destiny.

Seeing God's Stamp, Even on a Cynic

When we call people what God calls them, we identify God's stamp on their lives. These kinds of prophetic words can be very transformational. It's as if a new mirror gets put in front of them and they see themselves in a totally new perspective. When I see them as God sees them and call them as God calls them, they become what God created them to be.

I was in a foreign country several years ago ministering at a church. The pastor of the church had been praying for many years that his extended family would come to faith in Jesus. They were very skeptical, and his niece Linda was the most cynical of the bunch. Linda came to the Friday evening meeting ready to criticize and ridicule this prophet who had come from the United States. Before I began to speak, I went to her and gave her a word. "Linda, I see that you are a very strong willed person. You think creatively, and when you make a decision you stick to it. You are going to develop solutions to problems that people can't solve on their own. I see you with great compassion and wisdom. I see you studying banking and micro-finance. God will take you into third world countries, and you will help provide micro-financing in those countries."

She blankly stood there with no visible reaction. I continued to talk with her for about ten minutes, but there seemed to be no crack in her wall of cynicism. Later that night as I asked if anyone wanted to give their lives to Jesus, I was shocked that Linda came forward.

I didn't ever know the rest of the story until I went back to that church a couple years later. The pastor told me that during the time I had come previously, Linda was on holiday break from studying micro-finance in England. When I spoke the word to her, she knew it was God speaking to her. She had always wanted to go to third world countries to provide financial infrastructures for small businesses to flourish. Her parents worked in Africa for the World Health Organization. Linda had been raised there, and she had a dream to return.

Today, Linda is in Ghana providing micro-finance loans for start-up businesses, but she's doing it as a daughter of God. After she was saved, she played the recording of the prophetic word to her parents, and the whole family came to salvation in Jesus. God used that one word to stamp Linda with her true identity in Him, and a whole family was saved as a result. When God called her what He saw in her, she was empowered to become what He purposed her to be.

God's Breath

Then the Lord God formed a man from the dust of the ground and breathed into his nostrils the breath of life, and the man became a living being.
~ Genesis 2:7 (NIV)

God breathed on a pile of dirt. He knelt down from heaven to earth and breathed an intimate exhalation into the dust. His breath turned the mud-man into Adam and gave Adam life. The word for breath is the same word for Spirit. God breathed Himself into Adam and Eve. When God breathed on humanity, we took on the image and likeness of God (Gen. 1:27). When

Adam and Eve fell into sin, they lost the likeness of God. They had the spiritual breath knocked out of them.

That's the bad news. The good news is that Jesus came to put God's breath back into man. After His resurrection, Jesus came to His followers and said, "Receive the Holy Spirit" (John 20:22). Once again, divinity knelt down and touched humanity through breath. The breath they were created for was restored to them.

Seeing God's Breath in Others

Paul tells us in 1 Corinthians 12:6-11 that the Holy Spirit gives His gifts to the church, and one of those gifts is distinguishing between spirits. Literally, that means to distinguish the breath. This is a spirit-grace commonly called the discerning of spirits. It is one of the revelatory gifts and one of the least understood and most underutilized gifts we have been given.

Discerning of spirits is frequently understood as the ability to detect demonic influences. This is one working of the gift of discernment, but I would suggest that it is not the only use of the gift. We can also learn to discern God's breath in others.

 @bob_hazlett

The way U see what is temporal is with the eyes in your head. The way U see what is eternal is with the eyes of your heart. Eph. 1:18

Every human being has been marked with God's breath— the image of God's Spirit upon that person. We are each created uniquely, and we each reflect different aspects of God's breath. We distinguish what the breath of God looks, feels, and sounds like in that person. Even when they have had the breath knocked out of them, we can discern the fingerprint of God's image upon their lives. We can see the life and likeness of God in them even when they do not see it in themselves or act contradictory to it.

I once prophesied over a young boy. "You're the kind of kid who likes to hide a lot. You're sneaky!" The boy began to laugh, and so did his mom. I asked God to show me how this impression about hiding was a reflection of God's breath on the boy. "You really like to be alone, and God loves that about you," I continued. "When you go away and hide, those are times that God is really going to speak to you. Sometimes you talk to yourself, and people tell you not to do that, but really you're talking to God. He loves that about you."

I could tell that as I distinguished the breath of God in him, his mother started to see her son in a different light as well. Personality traits that she perceived as troublesome or negative and therefore needed to be suppressed suddenly came into a new light. She could see God's stamp on her son and how his quirks were a reflection of God's destiny upon his life.

Weakness + Breath = Strength

Another example of God pointing out His breath on someone's life is found in John chapter one. Jesus was recruiting disciples, and no one was less likely to become a disciple than Nathanael. He was a no-nonsense, tell-it-like-it-is guy who had a lot of skepticism when it came to Jesus.

> *Philip found Nathanael and told him, "We have found the one Moses wrote about in the Law, and about whom the prophets also wrote—Jesus of Nazareth, the son of Joseph."*
>
> *"Nazareth! Can anything good come from there?" Nathanael asked.*
>
> *"Come and see," said Philip.*
>
> *When Jesus saw Nathanael approaching, He said of him, "Here truly is an Israelite in whom there is no deceit."*
>
> *"How do you know me?" Nathanael asked.*

Jesus answered, "I saw you while you were still under the fig tree before Philip called you."

Then Nathanael declared, "Rabbi, you are the Son of God; you are the king of Israel."

Jesus said, "You believe because I told you I saw you under the fig tree. You will see greater things than that." He then added, "Very truly I tell you, you will see 'heaven open, and the angels of God ascending and descending on' the Son of Man."

~ John 1:45-51 (NIV)

The criticism and judgment were fresh off of Nathanael's lips when Jesus called him "a true Israelite in whom there is no deceit." Jesus could have pointed out the obvious sin, but instead, He used discernment of spirits to see the breath of God in Nathanael.

The breath of God in a person trumps anything they could ever say, do, or experience. We cannot define people by their actions, words, or attitudes. Rather, we look to God to see His breath upon them and call them as He sees them. When we do that, we empower them to become that person.

Jesus told Nathanael that he loved the truth. How could that be when Nathanael's last conversation had been to bash Jesus' ministry and hometown? But Jesus' words resounded profoundly with his heart, and Nathanael knew that there was something to what Jesus was saying. Jesus had just taken Nathanael's greatest weakness and added God's breath to it. The result was it called out Nathanael's hidden strength. Jesus had Nathanael's attention at that point.

Next, Jesus gave a word of knowledge: "I saw you sitting under a fig tree before Philip came to talk with you." There was no way Jesus could have known that, and this statement created a change in Nathanael's skeptical attitude. Jesus' words contained power and life. They held power to turn Nathanael's hard heart into a heart passionate for Jesus, and the result was that Nathanael was willing to lay down his life to follow Him.

Not only did the words reveal Nathanael to Nathanael, they also revealed Jesus to Nathanael. As Jesus identified God's breath upon Nathanael, Nathanael was able to see Jesus more clearly as well. "You are the son of God!" he exclaimed. Even though Nathanael's heart was already won over, Jesus went overboard by then speaking a destiny word over Nathanael to show Him God's plans for his life.

We must learn to distinguish the breath of God in others just as Jesus did with Nathanael. Proclamation of God's breath can transform a person's life, outlook, plans, and destiny in an instant.

One of the ways I practice seeing the breath of God in people is by beginning with the words, "You are the type of person who . . ." Then I begin to identify that person by the Spirit. Even if they have lost their breath, God can show me what they look like in the spirit with His breath. When people have a clear picture of how God sees them, they can more clearly see who God is.

Create, See, and Call

A pattern develops in Genesis 1. God creates something with His words, He sees it, and He names it. He creates light, sees it, and calls it day. He creates expanse between the waters, sees it, and calls it sky, and so on. In Genesis chapter two, the pattern changes. After God breathed His life into Adam, He did something mind-blowing:

> *Now the Lord God had formed out of the ground all the wild animals and all the birds in the sky. He brought them to the man to see what he would name them; and*

whatever the man called each living creature, that was its name. So the man gave names to all the livestock, the birds in the sky and all the wild animals.

~ Genesis 2:19-20 (NIV)

God amazingly chose to co-labor with the Spirit-infused Adam in the creation process. God created, but then He brought the animals to Adam so Adam could see them. Then He gave Adam the task of naming them. Before man was created, God named everything. After man was created, God chose to give this responsibility to Adam so they could partner together in the creative process. God empowered Adam to come into his destiny and purpose as one who sees as God sees and says what God says.

Again, the word for *see* here is *ra'ah*. Adam saw with discerning eyes into the animals. It wasn't a casual observation. He was able to see their purpose, their function, and their role. After he "*ra'ah*'d" them, he named them according to the purpose he saw in them. The act of naming created the animal's ability to become what God had created it to be. Whatever Adam called the creature was its name, and it then fulfilled its intended purpose. God created, but Adam saw and called, and then the animal became.

The conversation probably went something like this:

God: Adam, here's an animal I made. What do you see?

Adam: It looks like a good friend.

God: It needs a name.

Adam: I'm going to call it a dog.

Then the dog barked and became a dog.

God: Adam, here's another animal I made. What do you see?

Adam: It's strong and majestic. I'm going to call it a lion.

Then the lion roared and became a lion.

In Genesis 1, God modeled the prophetic process for us. He was the first to *ra'ah* and call destiny out based on what He saw. He is the ultimate seer. The stunning choice He made in Genesis 2 to then hand off the seeing and naming responsibility to man is sobering. God always intended to partner with man—those bearing His Spirit, image, and likeness—to see and name with Him.

 @bob_hazlett

Intimacy is the fuel for creativity. When U fall out of intimacy with God, life is dull. The closer U get 2 Him, the more creative U become!

Today, He continues to create. He is forming people's destinies, identities, and purposes for His glory. But He is also awaiting a people who will rise up and take their place as Spirit-filled image bearers who will once again see and name. He has modeled for us how to create, see, and name; now, He seeks those who will join Him on the journey to create, see, and name with Him.

The prophetic process is mirrored in the creative process depicted in Genesis 1 and 2. God created things, saw them for what He intended them to be, and named them according to His purposes. The prophetic process follows the same steps. God has already created people with His destiny and stamp placed upon them. Now, like Adam, it is our role to see them with discerning eyes. We are to recognize God's breath on them. Then we are to speak out and name that destiny God has placed within them. When we do that, we empower them to become what God has intended for them to become. We allow them to see themselves as they truly are and as they are not. As their

perceptions shift, they become transformed by the prophetic word, and they are empowered to live according to the destiny God has for them and to demonstrate to the world the breath of God that is within them.

What would happen if we started seeing the people around us as Adam saw? When you are having struggles with a spouse or family member, how would you treat them differently if you chose to see them through God glasses? What about your boss, co-workers, and neighbors? How would you respond to them differently? You could prophesy God's life and purposes into hopeless situations because you took the time to see as God sees and to say what God says.

Now consider how you would look at yourself and how you would speak to yourself if you were to see as God sees and speak as God speaks. I challenge you to look into a mirror today and to prophesy to yourself. Ask God to show you His breath within you. Look at yourself through God glasses, and see God's stamp upon you. Then speak the truth you see. As you speak it, it will empower you become who God truly created you to be.

CHAPTER 7
GOD'S SOUND RESTORES

"The yearning to know what cannot be known, to comprehend the incomprehensible, to touch and taste the unapproachable, arises from the image of God in the nature of man. Deep calleth unto deep, and though polluted and landlocked by the mighty disaster theologians call the Fall, the soul senses its origin and longs to return to its source."

—A.W. Tozer, The Pursuit of God

God's Sound Restores

Do Over

If you could go back and change one decision in your life, what would it be? I know what I would do. I would bring my bike inside the house on the night it was stolen.

I had the best bike in the neighborhood. It had front and back shocks and chrome all over. On that bike I could race the fastest, jump the farthest, and look the coolest of any kid on the street. I was almost immortal. That one decision brought me down to earth.

If Adam and Eve could change one decision, there is no question what it would be: eat the veggies, not the fruit! That decision brought a lot of things down to the earth. It brought sin, sickness, and death into an environment that was full of life.

I'm not sure how Adam and Eve looked physically before they sinned, but I imagine they were pretty awesome physical specimens. I like to envision Adam with six-pack abs and perfect hair. Eve was his perfect match. In an ageless environment, I picture them as forever twenty-one.

Before Adam and Eve ate of the forbidden fruit, they were perfect in every way: created in God's image, formed by God's hands, and stamped by His Spirit-breath. In one moment, everything changed. It was worse than having your bike stolen. It was having your body, soul, and spirit stolen all at once. It was the original identity theft.

Their fallen-spirit state caused them to lapse into spiritual death; they were no longer immortal. Their bodies must have changed because eventually they succumbed to disease, death, and decay. The change was possibly sudden, even immediate. Having read Bible stories my whole life, I've found ways to make them extra interesting. I visualize Adam's six pack dropping six inches and his forehead gaining those six inches. Eve? Well, let's just say sin took its toll.

Sin changed man's image. It was marred beyond recognition. A good picture of this is found in Isaiah 53:2-3 (NIV). Jesus was so beaten and bruised that "he had no beauty or majesty . . . like one from whom men hide their faces." In the same way that Jesus was disfigured physically, sin disfigured the image of God in man. Adam wanted to hide from God's face. Amazingly, Jesus' death restored the image of God in man, and we are now called God's children.

Sin also allowed the entrance of disease and death into the world through the Fall. Jesus suffered physically and atoned for sin and sickness on the cross. "By his wounds we are healed" (Is. 53:5, NIV). Jesus, the second Adam, came to restore everything the first Adam lost in the garden. His death and resurrection allow the rebirth of man in entirety: spirit, body, and soul.

God's Favorite Number

I am not sure if God has a favorite number—He created all of them—but I am pretty sure He really likes the number three. Look at all the threes in the Bible:

- Sun, moon, and stars make up the universe
- Father, Son, and Spirit make up the Godhead
- Abraham, Isaac, and Jacob make up the nation
- Outer court, inner court, and Holy of Holies make up the temple
- Body, soul, and spirit make up man

The trinitarian view of man reasons that just as God is triune, man has three parts. We are *spirit* beings who live in a *body* and have a *soul*. The soul allows us to reason, feel, and create. It makes sense that if man's sin caused his body to die and his spirit to die, it also impacted his soul. I believe, that man's abilities to think, feel, and desire were impacted by the Fall. The good news is Jesus came to give it all back. David celebrates that truth with these words: "He restores my soul" (Ps. 23:3, NKJV).

There are three faculties that can be attributed to the human soul: thinking (mind), feeling (emotions), and desire (will). Just as the body, soul, and spirit are distinct yet connected, the soul's functions are dependent on one another, even as they are distinct capacities.

The spirit of man was received when God's Spirit breathed into him, Spirit to spirit, breath to breath. The regenerated spirit has a direct connection to God. However there is a connection from the spirit of man to man's soul that is necessary for communication and prophetic function. A renewed mind, a restored soul, and a redeemed imagination are part of the finished work of Christ.

 @bob_hazlett

If you ever feel dispassionate for God, consider how passionate He is about you. There is never a dull moment in life!

The mind controls the intellectual capacities where we receive, store, and recall information. The emotions are governed by the conscience, which is the place where we perceive, feel, and establish bonds and boundaries with others. The will or desire function is found within the creative capacities of the soul. The Bible refers to this as the affections, or heart, of man. It is the place where our hopes are cultivated and our dreams are conceived; it is man's imagination.

God created the soul of man: mind, emotions, and will. In the same way that He formed man's body and released his spirit, God initiated man's ability to think, feel, and imagine. God's response when He saw this masterpiece was, "Awesome!" It was very good. Nothing God created is inherently evil or bad. The Fall of man caused everything to fall, including his soul. But the restored soul is powerful and necessary for understanding the supernatural, communing in the spirit, and creating God's intention on earth as it is in heaven. Maturing and being restored in the faculties of the soul will allow us to hear God's sound more clearly.

The writings of Rabbi Moses Maimonides are highly regarded by both Jewish and Christian theologians. His thoughts give insight to the Hebraic view of prophecy and the function of the soul in hearing God's sound:

> *PROPHECY is, in truth and reality, an emanation sent forth by the Divine Being through the medium of the Active Intellect, in the first instance to man's rational faculty, and then to his imaginative faculty; it is the highest degree and greatest perfection man can attain: it consists in the most Perfect development of the imaginative faculty.*[vii]

The prophetic process involves our whole being. God communicates to our spirit man, then our mind receives it, our conscience perceives it, and our imagination envisions it. If we put that in terms of physical senses, we would say the mind hears it, the conscience feels it, and the imagination sees it. A biblical portrait of this process is found in Isaiah 21:3 (NKJV):

> *Therefore my loins are filled with pain; pangs have taken hold of me, like the pangs of a woman in labor. I was distressed when I heard it; I was dismayed when I saw it.*

Isaiah received prophetic revelation, and it filtered through his soul. He saw it, he heard it, and he felt it—all the way down to his loins! But even Isaiah's soul did not experience the kind of pain that Adam and Eve felt when their soul fell. They were created with a mind that could receive divine communication, a conscience that allowed divine communion, and an imagination to release divine creativity. That was all about to change.

Looking in the Mirror

When the serpent came to Eve and tempted her with the fruit, he remarked, "When you eat of it, your eyes will be opened, and you will be like God" (Gen. 3:5). As always, the deceiver twisted things to his advantage. Man was already created in God's image, so they were already like God. They were able to see and speak from God's perspective because of who they were. The deception was that they had to do something more in order to be who they already were: "eat and you will be . . . " Religion is still selling that fruit, but I'm not buying it.

The true spiritual principle is taste and you will see (Ps. 34:8). Spiritual maturity or supernatural perception will not come through trying harder or performing better. It will only come when we "eat his flesh, and drink his blood" (see John 6:51-58).

When we understand Jesus' accomplishments on the cross and live in communion with God, it will change what and how we see. What you eat will impact how you perceive things. What you consume will determine your view. Adam and Eve tasted and they did not like what they saw. "Then the eyes of both of them were opened, and they knew that they were naked" (Gen. 3:7, NKJV).

When God saw (*ra'ah*) and called the light day, it became day. He felt good about that. When God formed an animal from the dirt and Adam saw (*ra'ah*) it, it became what he called it. That was good too. When man and woman sinned, they could see, but they could no longer *ra'ah*.

There are two Hebrew words for *see*. As we learned earlier, *ra'ah* is the God-kind of seeing. It's the ability to see through perception and discern through intention. The second kind of seeing is *yada*. It is to see by observation and to gain knowledge through experience. You could say when you *yada* something you look *at* it. When you *ra'ah* something you look *into* it. When man fell, he lost his ability to see like God; he could no longer perceive or discern. With his ability to see limited, it also distorted how man saw himself. All he could see when he looked at himself was the dirt and dust from which he came. His mirror was distorted.

It's interesting to note that the first thing man did when he sinned was to look at himself. He had been created by and for God. He had been given the greatest job in the world, to see and speak from God's perspective over what God created. He woke up every day to live for God and others. Then everything changed with the introduction of sin. Man embodied the greatest effect of sin: self-centeredness. Sin is selfish, self-indulgent, and focused on self-preservation.

Our sin is usually not a vicious plot to kick God off of His throne; it's mostly just a failure let Him rule our lives. It's about the trinity of me, myself, and I doing whatever seems right in my own eyes. Adam did what seemed right. But after he did it, it did not look, sound, or feel right any more.

Adam desperately attempted to cover up his mess. Fig leaves sound like pretty itchy underwear; sin will lead you to desperate measures. Sin affected the way Adam and Eve were able to see and also their ability to hear. When they heard God, they hid.

God would come every day for a visit. He would come with His sound and His Spirit. He would show up in the cool (*ruwach*: breath, spirit) of the day. The roar and *ruwach* of God is something God wanted them to hear and see. But they were naked and afraid, hidden and ashamed. The roar of God came to restore a fallen creation. He came to bring them out of hiding to tell them His intentions.

Who Told You that You Were . . . Oh My!

Please forgive me. I recognize that the story of original sin, the Fall of man, and the cursing of creation is a serious subject. It took a very serious event, the cross, to reverse its effects. But please allow me just one moment to at least snicker at the idea that man could hide this from God. God was not perplexed, seeking man's whereabouts. He was not playing hide and seek with Adam. He also wasn't sniffing out sin like a spiritual game of Marco Polo. He was doing what was in His nature: He came to seek and save that which was lost.

 @bob_hazlett

Courage is not the absence of fear, it's the knowledge that you are completely loved, accepted, and protected by God. Love drives away fear!

God's first words to fallen man are very important: "Where are you?" There were many alternatives He could have said. "What were you thinking? Why didn't you listen? Where did that underwear come from?" Instead, He decided His first sound to a sinful world would be, "Where have you been? I've been looking for you." Can you hear the roar? It's deep calling out to deep. It's love calling out to fear. It's destiny calling out to death. It's the sound of God in a raging a world.

Have you ever caught your child in the act of doing something wrong, and they tried to deny it? In the past, my wife would occasionally watch the two-year-old child of our friend. This child was very artistic and would use anything she found to draw with, especially things found in her diaper. I'm not kidding.

One day I was working in my office, and I heard the sound of the child waking. I thought I would help out my wife by getting the toddler from the crib. As I neared the room, I smelled the scent of sin. The child was naked and unashamed. She had just finished a self-portrait on my newly painted wall. What did I do? I did what any self-respecting man would do. I quietly left the room, went back to my desk, and called to my wife, "Honey, I think the baby might be awake."

After she cleaned the child, I came to see if I could assist. It took me a while to find my gas mask. The child looked at me, at the wall, and back to me before she said, "I didn't do it!" My wife and I looked at each other and tried not to crack a smile. We were still holding our breath! After we cleaned up the mess, we had a good laugh about it. I wonder if God ever wants to laugh at us, too.

It is preposterous to think some foliage and branches can cover original sin. There's a small part of me that pictures the edges of God's lips curling upward when Adam, fig leaves and fat hands trying to cover all his important parts, states, "I didn't do it!" The silliness of man's attempt to cover up turned into a sad attempt to tear down. "It was the *woman you* gave me" (Gen. 3:12). The Fall was complete: spiritual death, physical disease, and soul sickness.

Man was created to see what God could see and say what God would say, but the mind he was given to hear God's sound started to play tricks on him. Instead of hearing a loving Father, He heard a sound that made him fearful. The conscience he was given that allowed closeness and communion with the Almighty became shame-laden and guilt-ridden. He had to hide. Saddest of all, the ability to see and create with God had been perverted. He could no longer see God clearly. He looked at God and His creation, Eve, and declared them the problem.

I believe prophecy is not primarily intended to declare the problem in people, it is supposed to identify and release the potential in them. The Fall caused man to lose his mind, sear his conscience, and degrade his imagination. Prophecy under the Old Testament was mostly bad news. We cannot bring a New Covenant message with an Old Covenant perspective. We must view the Old Covenant through the eyes of the New Covenant.

Old Covenant Prophet, New Covenant Vision

When you have impaired vision, things don't look so good. As a twelve-year-old boy, the school nurse told me I needed glasses. For a year, I wore my glasses faithfully. My parents were just learning about divine healing, and my mother offered to pray for me. It was not a special prayer; in fact, she was making dinner at the time. As a result of her prayer, my vision returned to 20/20. The school nurse confirmed it!

The prophet Isaiah had vision problems also; all he prophesied in the first five chapters was bad news. In his defense, there were not a lot of good things happening. Here is sample of Isaiah's prophetic monologue. (You can decide if you would want him for your next motivational speaker or church revivalist.) He compares God's people donkeys. He says they will live in a hole in the ground. He proclaims they will have a stench that would reach to heaven. Wait! Here is some good news. They will have a big mansion, a private vineyard, and throw lavish parties. However, the mansion will be empty, the vineyard will be barren, and the party guests will die of thirst and starvation.

Something dramatic happened in chapter six. God expanded Isaiah's vision to see more clearly from a heavenly view. He was given corrective lenses. His vision was enlarged by a vision of God, high and exalted, seated on a throne surrounded by terrifying angels. This vision allowed Isaiah to then have a clearer understanding of heaven, the character and majesty of God, and His intentions on the earth. The encounter changed him forever.

We may not have the same encounter Isaiah did, but we have something even better: Jesus. Jesus came to earth to show us who God is. Jesus said, "If you have seen me, you have seen my Father. If you have heard my words, you have heard my Father" (see John 14:9-10). That is a powerful statement. Jesus came to show us what God looks and sounds like. Jesus put skin on God.

I believe we as prophetic people get to show others what Jesus looks and sounds like. The apostle John, perhaps the human being who spent the most time with Jesus outside of His mother, said prophecy is the testimony of Jesus (Rev. 19:10). It is the spoken record of what Jesus looks like. Jesus was the Word that became flesh. Just as Jesus put skin on God, prophecy puts skin on Jesus. I want to see Jesus so people can see Jesus in me! I want to hear Jesus so people can hear Jesus through me! I want to know Jesus so people can get to know Jesus too.

During Isaiah's visionary experience recorded in Isaiah 6, he was really introduced to God. If you want to see someone, you can invite them over to your house. If you want to really know someone, you need to visit them where they live. You should meet their family, smell their cooking, sit at their table, and taste their food. Isaiah visited God, and he did not like what he saw:

> *"Woe to me!" I cried. "I am ruined! For I am a man of unclean lips, and I live among a people of unclean lips, and my eyes have seen the King, the Lord Almighty."*
> ~ *Isaiah 6:5 (NIV)*

When Isaiah saw God in heaven, he called Him the king, choosing messianic language. The Apostle John verified that Isaiah's vision was of Jesus (John 12:41). God gave Isaiah a vision of Jesus, and it changed him forever. Jesus is the visible image of the invisible God.

After Isaiah saw Jesus, God sent a seraph with coals that literally burned the sin and guilt out of Isaiah. "See, this has touched your lips, your guilt is taken away, your sin is atoned for" (Is. 6:7, NIV). He tasted and then He saw that the Lord is good!

I believe God allowed Isaiah to see the atonement process before the cross so he could describe it prophetically for those of us who would walk after the cross. Not surprisingly, Isaiah reveals more about Jesus than any other Old Covenant prophet. He had a testimony of Jesus, and all of Isaiah's messianic prophecies occurred after Isaiah 6. He became an Old Covenant prophet with a New Covenant perspective.

Custom-Made Clothing

I am not a big fan of shopping. That is my wife's spiritual gift. I usually go online if I need to buy something. Not long ago, a friend offered to take me shopping for a custom suit. "Can we do it online?" I asked.

"No, you have to fly to Miami. That is where the shop is," he responded. I thought it was strange to fly from New York to Miami to go clothes shopping when I go to the mall maybe twice per year. I was able to work out a four-hour layover in Miami on a trip back from the West Coast. When I landed, I did what I normally do: I texted my wife and told her where I was.

"Why are you connecting in Miami to come to New York?" she asked.

"Clothes shopping," I replied.

"Whoever this is, give the phone back to my husband!" she demanded.

The suit came out great. I didn't wear suits often in the past. Most places I speak are business casual. But I wear this suit every chance I get! Even if I am speaking at a casual dress conference, I sometimes wear it just for the airplane, and then it hangs in my hotel closet. Why? Because it was made just for me. Also, it cost my friend a lot of money. He wanted to show how much he valued me by giving me something costly. I want to show him how much I appreciate his gift by wearing it as much as possible.

I will let you in on another secret: people treat me nice when I wear that suit. I call it my upgrade suit. I know who I am with jeans on, but when other people see the suit, they see me differently. They see who I really am.

When Adam and Eve sinned, they couldn't see who they really were any more. God had to do something about that. He made them a suit. It was not custom made. It was one size fits all. It was costly, though, at least for the animal that had to give its life for Adam and Eve's mistake. It required the shedding of the innocent blood of an animal.

Imagine how they felt watching God slit its throat and drain the blood. They knew this animal. God had presented it to Adam in the garden and he had named it. They saw and spoke its purpose into being. Now they were watching as God skinned it so their naked flesh could be clothed. The suit did not cover their sin. It only served as a reminder of what they had done. I can imagine each day as they would put on their suit, they clothed their flesh with animal flesh and shed a tear for the life that was taken so their life could continue—that is, if you call that living.

That is a picture of life under the Old Covenant. The law was a one-size-fits-all moral code designed to expose the weakness of flesh. God gave one rule in the garden and man broke it. God followed that by ten rules on a mountain. Ironically, they were all being broken at the same time God was writing them.

From Adam on, sin was always in the picture, but the law brought it into focus. The law showed us we were all guilty. Even a new suit could never solve man's sin problem. Just like the animal skin on Adam's flesh, the law is just a reminder of sin.

Perfection Required, Relationship Restored

A custom tailored suit takes a lot of preparation. I did not know that. You have to have an advance appointment. You can't just drop by any time. You have to pick a special fabric from a special book. You have to choose buttons and linings. Those buttons and linings have to match the fabric. You have to wear the right shoes, the right socks, the right shirt, and the right belt when they measure you. If you don't do it just right, if you make one mistake, the measurements will be off and you will be forever banished from the custom suit process. Not really, but it does feel a little bit like you are trying to qualify for something rather than being given a gift. That is an apt description of the sacrificial system of the law.

Under the Old Covenant, once per year the high priest made an appointment called the Day of Atonement. It was the day when an animal would be sacrificed for the sin of the people. Everything had to be right. He had to have the right suit, the right belt, the right shoes, even the right perfume. He had to pray right, talk right, and walk right. The goal was to make it into the Holy of Holies, sprinkle the blood on the mercy seat, and get out without making a mistake. If the priest did any component incorrectly, he would be forever banished—as in dead. Nothing that was unholy could come into God's presence in the most holy place. If anything was wrong with the animal, priest, or his suit, he would die. Even when he did everything just right, it would still have to be done over and over and over (Heb. 10:11).

 @bob_hazlett

Criticism comes from the accuser. Conviction comes from the Spirit of truth. I never listen to the accuser, nor do I want to be his echo.

They had a lot of do-overs, but they never qualified. Jesus came to give us a gift. This is a once for all, all expenses paid, custom made new creation: body, soul, and spirit. The writer of Hebrews spoke of Jesus' works:

> *But when this priest had offered for all time one sacrifice for sins, he sat down at the right hand of God, and since that time he waits for his enemies to be made his footstool. For by one sacrifice he has made perfect forever those who are being made holy.*
> *~ Hebrews 10:12-14 (NIV)*

What was lost in the garden was restored on the cross. An annual reminder has become an eternal celebration. Sin lost. Jesus won. You are no longer naked and ashamed, no longer hidden and afraid. No fig leaves or finger pointing are necessary.

Why is this important in a book about hearing God's sound? What does Hebrews 10 have to do with prophecy? You were created to see what God sees, hear His sound, and say what He says. That was lost in the garden. Your spiritual senses, which operate through the intellect, emotions, and imagination, were impaired. The mind, heart, and conscience of man were damaged. Animal skin and stone tablet laws could not repair them.

As the familiar song says:

What can wash away my sin?
Nothing but the blood of Jesus.
What can make me whole again?
Nothing but the blood of Jesus.

Hebrews also explains to us that when Jesus died, He walked through the more perfect tabernacle than the priests of the Old Covenant (Heb. 9:11). His blood did not only cleanse our sin and heal our bodies, it made us whole: spirit, body, and soul.

> *He [the Holy Spirit] says, "This is the covenant I will make with them after that time, says the Lord. I will put my laws in **their hearts**, and I will write them on **their minds**." Then he adds, "Their sins and lawless acts I will remember no more." And where these have been forgiven, sacrifice for sin is no longer necessary.*

> *Therefore, brothers and sisters, since we have confidence to enter the Most Holy Place by the blood of Jesus, by a new and living way opened for us through the curtain, that is, his body, and since we have a great priest over the house of God, let us draw near to God with a sincere heart and with the full assurance that faith brings, having our hearts sprinkled **to cleanse us from a guilty conscience** and having our bodies washed with pure water.*
> *~ Hebrews 10:15-22 (NIV; emphasis added)*

New Conscience, Mind, and Imagination

Christ's atoning works accomplished much, and through Him we are offered a clean conscience, a renewed mind, and a redeemed imagination.

You were born with a guilty conscience, but in Christ you have been given a clean conscience. When we hear God's sound, we no longer run from it and hide; we run toward it. With great confidence we enter the most holy place. The Apostle John was bold in his faith, and even bolder in drawing near to Jesus' heart. He said, "Beloved, if our heart does not condemn us, we have confidence toward God" (1 John 3:21, NKJV). Condemnation will keep you from hearing God's heart. Jesus' blood has cleansed you from a guilty conscience, just as when Isaiah's lips were touched by the coal. With a clean conscience, your prayers will be bolder, God's sound will be sharper, and communion will be sweeter.

 @bob_hazlett

The fear of man is rooted in comparison. The fear of God is rooted in the fact that He is beyond comparison!

Not only was your conscience cleansed, but Jesus' works gave us a new mind as well: the mind of Christ. Your mind was given for you to learn and understand the mysteries of heaven. When Adam heard God's sound in the garden, fear played tricks on his mind. Supernatural sounds are fearful to those without a renewed mind. When I was a child I had repeated nightmares, audible voices in my room, and things physically attacked me in my bed. Fear caused me to shut down those voices. I turned off the circuit breaker to the supernatural.

When God's sound roared into my life in Pensacola, Florida, in June of 1997, that switch got turned back on. That night in my hotel, I again heard voices and had visitations, but it was of the heavenly kind. Some people would say that I needed deliverance prayer as a child; I would say I needed identity prayer. When the switch got turned back on, I remembered heavenly voices I had shut out as a child and spiritual experiences I had forgotten. Fear caused me to focus on what the devil was doing instead of what God was doing.

I am convinced that many children that have night terrors and nightmares are prophetic in nature, and the devil wants to cause them to turn off the supernatural circuit breaker out of fear. Maybe they need deliverance, or maybe they need someone to remind them who they are like Paul did for Timothy:

> *Therefore I remind you to stir up the gift of God which is in you through the laying on of my hands. For God has not given us a spirit of fear, but of power and of love and of a sound mind.*
>
> *~ 2 Timothy 1:6-7 (NKJV)*

I have seen many people healed of mind disorders by this truth. In one example, someone with dyslexia so severe that he had to read his Bible upside down and backward had to flip his Bible the right way when God flipped the switch.

Jesus also touches our imaginations and brings them back to life. Hope is the engine that runs an imagination. The way that engine is wired will determine what future you drive to. When wired to an earthly perspective, hope turns to worry and drives you to your greatest fears. When wired to a heavenly perspective, the engine of hope creates the future reality God intends.

When man looked at dirt and dust in the form of animals and named them, he had hope that something would happen. He expected God to empower his words and accomplish what he said. When he lost hope, his words shifted to negative predictions, fault finding, and blame shifting. He was worried that God was mad and would do something bad. A guilty conscience and fearful mind created a lack of hope. Let God re-wire your imagination. Follow Paul's advice to the Colossian church:

> *Since, then, you have been raised with Christ, set your hearts on things above, where Christ is, seated at the*

> *right hand of God. Set your minds on things above, not on earthly things.*
>
> *~ Colossians 3:1-2 (NIV)*

The word heart used here reflects affections or desires. Let God rewire your heart to heaven. Let your imagination be redeemed. What can make you whole again? Nothing but the blood of Jesus!

Redeemed Soul

There was a teaching in Paul's day called Gnosticism. Gnosticism was a Greek philosophy that taught that matter was evil and the spirit was good. This teaching promoted a clear separation between the material and spiritual worlds. True Christian doctrine became mingled with Gnosticism in some churches, resulting in a twisted view of Jesus. Christian Gnostics said since matter was evil, God could not really take on human flesh. He only seemed to possess a human form and only appeared to suffer; it was an illusion. This was human reasoning, a way that seemed right to man, but not truth. The Gnostics also taught that man is composed of body, soul, and spirit. However, they believed that the body and the soul are man's earthly existence and are considered evil. This couldn't be further from biblical truth. However, residue of this type of thinking still creeps into the church today.

If we believe the body and soul are evil, it may keep us from experiencing God in our whole being. David said, "My soul thirsts for you, my flesh longs for you" (Ps. 63:1, NKJV). He wanted to experience God in his whole being. We are in the process of being sanctified in our whole being as Paul stated:

Now may the God of peace Himself sanctify you
completely; and may your whole spirit, soul, and body be
preserved blameless at the coming of our Lord Jesus
Christ.

~ *1 Thessalonians 5:23 (NKJV)*

Just as you can be experiencing physical sickness and still be used by God to heal the sick, you can be in the process of having your soul restored and still hear Him and see Him. A completely healed body is not a prerequisite for laying hands on the sick. Belief that God will use you to heal others, even as you are being healed is the essence of faith. Allow God to sanctify your soul and allow Him to use you to bring words that will restore the ability for others to see as God sees and say what God says.

God's Sound or My Soul?

There is one question I am asked more than any other about prophetic ministry and hearing God's voice: "Is what I am hearing God or me?" My answer is always the same: Yes! After a short pause to let that sink in, I usually explain more. Hearing God is always God and me, because communication takes two people. I understand that what they want to know is, "How can I know if what I am sensing, seeing, and hearing is coming from God, my own feelings, or some other source?"

I appreciate the intent behind the question. We should have a desire for excellence in prophetic ministry and clarity in hearing God. Excellence is a value of the kingdom of God. However, perfectionism is not. Perfectionism is rooted in fear and it tells us we must do it right or not at all. Excellence realizes we can always grow, constantly learn, and the kingdom is always advancing. Perfectionism can cause fear of failure, which paralyzes the faith necessary to take risk. Prophecy, as with all spiritual gifts, works by faith, and faith works by love and never in accordance with fear. This is why I have a simple prayer I pray every day, before each meeting, in every city, nation, and church I minister to: "God help me to love the way you love, see only what you see, and say only what you say." His love removes all fear. Love answers many questions.

As we have seen, God has a role in prophecy and I have a role in prophecy. It is received in my spirit, and I process it through my spiritual senses in my soul. The question remains: what is the source? The book of James gives helpful instruction on the sources of wisdom and how to discern its source.

> *Who is wise and understanding among you? Let them show it by their good life, by deeds done in the humility that comes from wisdom. But if you harbor bitter envy and selfish ambition in your hearts, do not boast about it or deny the truth. Such "wisdom" does not come down **from heaven but is earthly, unspiritual, demonic**. For where you have envy and selfish ambition, there you find disorder and every evil practice. But the wisdom that comes from heaven is first of all pure; then peace-loving, considerate, submissive, full of mercy and good fruit, impartial and sincere. Peacemakers who sow in peace reap a harvest of righteousness.*
> *~ James 3:13-18 (NIV; emphasis added)*

The human soul processes input from all these sources: heavenly, earthly, unspiritual, and demonic. It is similar to water passing through filters to remove impurities, except it's the opposite. What we receive from God is pure, and the filters can add something not intended. This is why having the soul restored by God is so important. Holding on to hurt from past experience, the bitterness of offense, and selfish ambition will put filters in the soul that make it hard to discern clearly. A word that comes from heaven can go through a filter of experience, and personal opinion enters in, clouding the word. It then passes through a filter of offense, and unspiritual feelings enter in. It may even pass a filter of personal ambition, which could result in spiritual control, which is demonic. Let me illustrate this for you.

Many years ago while on the pastoral team of a church, I was training a group of people in prayer. I was doing prophetic ministry, but I had not yet begun teaching on prophecy. One particular woman spent a lot of time in prayer and consistently seemed to hear God clearly. She also demonstrated a humble heart to learn. One day, she approached me and told me God had spoken to her something for the church and the senior pastor. I told her to write it down, and I would read it with the pastor and get back to her. I thought this would be a good learning experience. It turned out that it was, especially for me.

The letter she wrote started very respectfully. She said that she saw God growing the church in the area of discipleship. This seemed like it was from God because they were planning a new emphasis on discipleship. Next, she said that part of the discipleship would include a ministry of physical and emotional healing gifts because many of the church leaders needed emotional healing. We raised an eyebrow as we read it. While it was true that healing was part of the discipleship plan, her personal opinion based on past experience with leaders caused a mixture.

Then things got strange. She said that if we did not have a ministry of healing, the church would have a division because so many people needed healing that they would go somewhere else. She finished by saying, "I command that you put so-and-so as the leader of the healing ministry." The progression was clear. She started out hearing from above, then from earth, and then from an unspiritual feeling, then from a spiritual control that was clearly not God. This did not cause us any confusion or fear. We as leaders knew what was God and what was not God. We knew how to rightly divide the word of truth. But I had to respond.

My choice, as a leader, was to either demand perfection or to encourage excellence. If perfection was the goal, she failed, and many would say she could never hear from God again. However, because excellence was the pursuit, my response was to help her grow. The pursuit toward excellence was up to her. I shared my impressions with her and showed her where she got off track. She humbly received correction. The way I corrected her brought healing from past events when leaders corrected her harshly. As a result, she let go of that hurt. Her soul was being healed. I told her that I wanted her to spend the next month reading the Bible and not giving any prophecies. I encouraged her to read James because it talks about wisdom and maturity. I was not punishing her for being a bad prophetess; I was helping her become a better one. I believe that if we are going to be people that speak God's words, we must be people who know and become God's Word. It needs to be planted in us so we can grow.

 @bob_hazlett

If what you hear the Holy Spirit speak produces guilt and shame, you are hearing Him in the wrong tone, or what you are hearing is not Him.

God has given you a soul with which to receive from Him and respond to Him. James admonishes us,

> *So then, my beloved brethren, let every man be swift to hear, slow to speak, slow to wrath; for the wrath of man does not produce the righteousness of God. Therefore lay aside all filthiness and overflow of wickedness, and receive with meekness the **implanted word, which is able to save your souls**. But be doers of the word, and not hearers only, deceiving yourselves.*
> *~ James 1:19-22 (NKJV)*

God implants His words deep into the soil of our lives. As it grows, it brings salvation to our souls. It brings restoration. He paid for your soul's restoration with a costly price, the death of Jesus. 2 Corinthians 5 says that when Christ died, all died. Allow hurt, offense, and selfish ambition to die, and walk in new life! Be slow to speak and quick to hear. Allow God's word to be implanted in you so your soul will be made whole.

I can see a company of people who walk in their God-given identity. They are slow to speak but bold to proclaim. They walk in humility that comes from wisdom; selfish ambition has no hold on them. Their senses are keen, and their discernment is sharp. They can see what God sees and say what God says. Their souls magnify the Lord; their spirits rejoice in God!

CHAPTER 8
THE DNA OF GOD'S SOUND

"The cross is not responsible for God's love; rather it was His love which conceived the cross as the one method by which we could be saved. God felt no different toward us after Christ had died for us, for in the mind of God Christ had already died before the foundation of the world. God never saw us except through atonement. The human race could not have existed one day in its fallen state had not Christ spread His mantle of atonement over it. And this He did in eternal purpose long ages before they led Him out to die on the hill above Jerusalem. All God's dealings with man have been conditioned upon the cross."

—A.W. Tozer, The Radical Cross: Living the Passion of Christ

The DNA of God's Sound

God's Sound Heals

My friend Steve is an amazing musician, worship leader, and prophetic psalmist. He can make sounds that I have rarely heard come from a keyboard, and he can create spontaneous songs in a moment. He is like a supernatural sound machine. We were ministering together once at a conference, and I was doing a prophetic exercise. Somehow we got partnered up for this one. He showed me a picture of a little girl that he carries in his wallet. "Her name is Rachel. What do you see about her?" he asked.

As I looked at the picture, I saw a hand coming down from heaven and it rested on her head. Then I heard singing. I thought about the scripture that says, "I hear Rachel weeping for her children" (Jer. 31:15).

I said, "Rachel is not weeping; she is singing. She likes to sing the songs you write. Her life is going to turn weeping children to into singing children. I see a hand on her head, and I believe it means that God is going to give you songs that will heal brain injuries and change genetic structures that will result in creative miracles. Children who have brain injuries and incomplete DNA will be healed as a result of your songs."

You have to know Steve to picture his face. He has the biggest smile that never seems to fade. He was smiling through his tears as he told the story of Rachel. She had died of a brain tumor. Steve had visited her many times and sang over her, believing God would heal her. She would sing along with him. There was an understandable sadness in his eyes at the death of this child, but a joyful reassurance in his smile that the sounds

God gave him were being sung in heaven and the sounds that originated in heaven would bring healing on the earth. God's sound heals!

God's Sound in the DNA

Several years ago, I came across an interesting research study done by a group from Harvard Medical School and M.I.T. regarding the sound that could be obtained from the DNA sequence taken from human blood samples. Research fellow Gil Alterovitz at M.I.T. and Harvard Medical School has developed a computer program that translates information about cells' gene and protein expressions into musical sequences.[viii]

After stripping away the scientific lingo, here is how the study worked and what surprised them. They converted specific nucleotides, the raw material of DNA, into specific notes. Next, after taking blood samples from several participants, they programmed their DNA into the translator. They found what they expected; different genetic sequences produced different sounds. Every person has a completely unique DNA, so they produced completely unique sounds.

What surprised them was that the genetic sequence not only produced sound, in every case it produced a melody. In each person's genetic structure there is a sound, a unique melodious song right in the blood! I am not sure what my blood song sounds like, but I am pretty sure it's not hip-hop.

Here is the other surprising thing they discovered. More than one participant suffered with cancer, and the sound of the DNA was different in a specific way. "The normal patients relative to the baseline sound harmonic," Alterovitz explained, "whereas [with] the cancer patients, it sounds more inharmonious." The blood song in the cancer patient was a disharmonious sound. The cancer did not belong.

Jesus Has a Blood Song

There is a song in your blood. You can hear it by sending a sample of your blood to a company who will extract the DNA and produce a song for you, fully orchestrated for an extra fee.[ix] Once again science has proven what the Bible said over two thousand years ago: the blood speaks!

> *But you have come to Mount Zion, to the city of the living God, the heavenly Jerusalem. You have come to thousands upon thousands of angels in joyful assembly, to the church of the firstborn, whose names are written in heaven. You have come to God, the Judge of all, to the spirits of the righteous made perfect, to Jesus the mediator of a new covenant, **and to the sprinkled blood that speaks a better word than the blood of Abel.***
>
> *~ Hebrews 12:22-24 (NIV; emphasis added)*

There is currently a cultural fixation with blood—vampire books and movies, gothic clothing, and even drinks made to look like you are drinking blood. It's all a little too dark for me. I am not alarmed by it because I understand something: the devil has no power to create; he can only copy.

Several years ago, the church stopped talking about blood and ghosts and crosses. We were trying to attract the lost. I understand the need to be culturally relevant, and I'm also a strong proponent in updating our language so it is not a barrier. My suggestion is that we make the blood understandable to spiritual seekers. Make the Holy Sprit accessible, and make the cross a symbol of celebration. If darkness can make blood culturally relevant, then children of the light need not be ashamed of it either.

Jesus' blood has a sound—a roar! It is the first and best song ever written. It is wedding song of bride. It is the anthem of the winning team. It is the song that never ends. Jesus' blood tells you where you come from. Isaiah visited heaven, but you have been born from heaven if you have been born again.

Jesus is a master teacher. He knows that the best way to teach is not by answering every question but by getting His students to ask the right questions. Nicodemus was called Israel's teacher, but Jesus took him to school in John 3:

> *Now there was a Pharisee, a man named Nicodemus who was a member of the Jewish ruling council. He came to Jesus at night and said, "Rabbi, we know that you are a teacher who has come from God. For no one could perform the signs you are doing if God were not with him."*
>
> *Jesus replied, "Very truly I tell you, no one can see the kingdom of God unless they are born again."*
>
> *"How can someone be born when they are old?" Nicodemus asked. "Surely they cannot enter a second time into their mother's womb to be born!"*
>
> *Jesus answered, "Very truly I tell you, no one can enter the kingdom of God unless they are born of water and the Spirit. Flesh gives birth to flesh, but the Spirit gives birth to spirit."*
>
> *~ John 3:1-6 (NIV)*

Nicodemus didn't come to Jesus because He was a good preacher or because he could draw big crowds. He came to Jesus because he knew Jesus came *from* God. How did he know this? Because of the miraculous signs He performed. He was attracted to Jesus' understanding and authority, and he considered Jesus' ministry valid because of the supernatural manifestation that followed it. His miracles proved where He had come from.

Jesus' next statement brought the question to Nicodemus' lips that every preacher in modern history has been trying to get people to ask: How can I be born again? Jesus replied, "You can not see the kingdom of God unless you are born again." Another way to translate this is "born from above." If want to see heaven, you have to be born from heaven.

Birth is a bloody experience. I know because I have watched two of them. I tried to avoid the bloody parts. Nicodemus wanted no part of getting back into that. "You cannot go back to your mother's womb," he rebuffed.

"Of course not," Jesus said. "Flesh gives birth to flesh, and Spirit gives birth to spirit."

Conception is an intimate thing. When a man enters a woman, it is a holy event. When it happens for the first time, blood is shed. When Jesus entered the most holy place with His blood, He had to pass through the curtain, which is His body. He sprinkled the blood on the mercy seat in the most holy place. When He did, He impregnated heaven with the church, the church of the first-born.

Heaven was pregnant with you before the foundation of the world. You were chosen in Christ before anything was spoken into existence. How is that possible since Jesus died two thousand years ago on a cross on earth? It is possible because when Jesus entered heaven with His blood, He was no longer in the dimension of time and space; He was in eternity. That is why He is called the Lamb slain from the foundation of the world (Rev. 13:8). His blood is the first song because it was shed first. Before there was any blood, His blood was speaking.

When you are born again, you are not getting a second chance at being a better human being; you are given your first chance at being a heavenly being. You are not an earthly being trying to live a spiritual life; you are a spirit being in a fleshly body living a heavenly culture in an earthly environment every day. The cross was not your chance for a do-over. It was your first chance to live the life you were created to live.

The Blood that Triumphs

Some people have experienced sibling rivalry, but not me! Maybe it's because I am fourth out of five in birth order and the first male. My sisters spoiled me. I never had to compete for anything, except the bathroom.

That was not the case with the two first born of the first creation. Those who were born of the flesh and into sin continued to live in that fallen state. Abel and his brother Cain competed. Abel won favor with God, but lost his life at the hands of his jealous brother. Abel was the first born of the first creation to have his blood spilled. It was taken unjustly, and it cried out for justice. God told Cain, "The voice of your brother's blood cries out to Me from the ground" (Gen. 4:10, NKJV).

His blood was speaking, and it was not a good sound. It called out the guilt of Cain. It cried for judgment; it roared for revenge. God takes blood very seriously. It is what gave life to the soul of man, and it carried the image of God in man's flesh.

> *But you shall not eat flesh with its life, that is, its blood. Surely for your lifeblood I will demand a reckoning; from the hand of every beast I will require it, and from the hand of man. From the hand of every man's brother I will require the life of man. "Whoever sheds man's blood, By man his blood shall be shed; For in the image of God He made man."*
>
> *~ Genesis 9:4-6 (NKJV)*

When you murder someone, you are saying their soul has no value, and you destroy the image of God in them. That is serious stuff. Jesus rephrased this for us in the Sermon on the Mount:

You have heard that it was said to the people long ago,
"You shall not murder, and anyone who murders will be
subject to judgment." But I tell you that anyone who is
angry with a brother or sister will be subject to
judgment. Again, anyone who says to a brother or sister,
"Raca," is answerable to the court. And anyone who says,
"You fool!" will be in danger of the fire of hell.

~ Matthew 5:21-22 (NIV)

The fire of hell! That is strong language. Apparently so is the word *fool* to Jesus. Jesus is fired up about how we use words because He understands that the power of life and death is in the tongue (Prov. 18:21). When we tear people down with our words, we are tearing down God's image in them. When we diminish people through criticism, gossip, and hateful speech, we devalue the soul. In God's eyes, it is like murdering them.

 @bob_hazlett

If you would not think it or say it in front of God, you probably
should not think about it or say it at all. Psalm 19:14

This might be a good moment to pause and repent. That means to change your mind about something. When Peter was preaching on the day of Pentecost, he reminded the people of how they killed the Messiah: "and you, with the help of wicked men, put him to death by nailing him to the cross" (Acts 2:23, NIV). He was telling them that they were responsible for the blood of the Son of God, and they understood (Acts 2:37). They were cut to the heart. They must have thought, "That's it, we're toast! We killed the Messiah!"

Peter said, "Don't worry; there is a solution. Repent, change your mind, and be baptized" (see Acts 2:28). Welcome to the church of the firstborn!

The blood of Jesus speaks a better word than the blood of Abel (Heb. 12:24). Abel's blood cried, "guilty." Jesus' blood responded, "not guilty." Abel's blood screamed for revenge. Jesus' blood roared, "Mercy triumphs over judgment" (James 2:13).

The Song of the Bride

Every girl dreams of her wedding, and every dad dreads the thought of it. At least this dad does. There is one thing about that day that I look forward to. Well, maybe two, if you count handing off the college debt. The first thing, though, is the father-daughter dance. I think about that. I imagine it. I plan on capturing the moment forever when it happens.

The devil messed up the first creation song. Because of that, Adam and Eve were responsible for the blood of the first animal killed, and their son was responsible for the blood of Abel. Theirs were the first unjust bloodshed in the first creation. Now there is a new creation and a church of the firstborn. There is a new song: the song of the bride.

After the cross, the devil wanted to stop the music and do his dance again. How? By shedding innocent blood. Stephen became the first martyr of the church of the firstborn. His blood was shed unjustly. He looked into an open heaven while men stood angrily with rocks in their hands. He prayed, "Father, forgive them," while they hurled accusations at him:

> *Yelling at the top of their voices, they all rushed at him, dragged him out of the city and began to stone him. Meanwhile, the witnesses laid their coats at the feet of a young man named Saul. While they were stoning him, Stephen prayed, "Lord Jesus, receive my spirit." Then he fell on his knees and cried out, "Lord, do not hold this sin against them."*
>
> *~ Acts 7:57-60 (NIV)*

Instead of seeing and speaking from an earthly perspective, Stephen saw heaven and spoke heaven's language. Rather than returning accusation for accusation and stone for stone, he blessed those who cursed him. He could have held them accountable for his blood, but instead, he spoke a better word. Rather than agreeing with the blood of Abel, he chose to agree with the blood of Jesus. His words had the power of life, and God heard his words.

Just a few days later, Saul, the same man who was collecting coats and distributing stones at Stephen's execution, was on his way to spill more blood in Damascus. But something happened. He saw and heard something unlike any sight or sound you would hear on earth. It came straight from heaven. It was the sound of God calling his name. It was the light of God revealing Himself to Saul.

What made the deep of heaven call out to Saul's deep? What caused the light of heaven to pierce Saul's darkness? I have to believe it was the prayer of Stephen. It was his blood crying out, "Mercy!"

That cry released a light and a sound from heaven that turned the murderous Saul into to Apostle Paul. An abuser was turned into a father of the Church. An accuser was transformed into the writer of love letters from God to His bride. That is the power of the blood of the Lamb.

Prophecy and the Blood

While Stephen stood being stoned, he saw heaven opened and he spoke. What you see will determine what you will say. Because he chose God's perspective, he spoke God's purpose. Instead of watching his accusers, Stephen was watching God. In that moment, he became a watchman and a spokesman for heaven on earth.

Ezekiel, the prophet, was also a watchman (Ezek. 33:1-6). The word means "one who is a witness between two parties." In fact, God tells Ezekiel, "I will hold the watchman accountable for their blood" (Ezek. 33:6, NKJV). Ezekiel was a witness between God and Israel, and he witnessed some terrible sights. As a prophet, his willingness or unwillingness to share God's words was directly linked to the blood of those he was to watch over.

Have you ever been called for jury duty? I was once. I was happy I did not get picked. Just getting the letter can be a little unnerving. In a society of laws, we need judgments and punishments. However, even when the person is guilty and deserves judgment, few people desire to be the one to stand up in front of the world and pronounce the verdict. However, that is exactly what a watchman does. God emphasized the role of watchman when He warned Ezekiel, "You are responsible for their blood." I would rather have jury duty.

The fact is that God has made each of us a watchman. We watch over those God has placed in our lives. We remind them of the blood that already paid for them and encourage them to live up to that standard. As watchmen, we are responsible to see and speak what the blood of Jesus says about a person, city, or nation. When the enemy comes against them, we get to stand with God for them. We get to declare the verdict of heaven: "Not guilty."

A Prophetic Blessing

The first words recorded in the Bible from God toward man gave man identity. It was the sound of heaven that impacted earth.

Then God blessed them, and God said to them, "Be fruitful and multiply; fill the earth and subdue it; have

*dominion over the fish of the sea, over the birds of the
air, and over every living thing that moves on the earth."*
~ Genesis 1:28 (NKJV)

Adam and Eve were blessed by God to be agents of
blessing to the world. With God's blessing of Adam in Genesis
1:28, we see a pattern of three components to prophetic
blessings: increase ("be fruitful and multiply"), influence ("fill the
earth and subdue it"), and inheritance ("have dominion").

Prophecy and blessing are connected throughout the
scripture, not just with Adam and Eve. In fact, the given name
to a person at birth was a prophetic blessing. Adam's name
means to show blood in the face, according to Strong's
Concordance of Hebrew words item number 119. From the
beginning, Adam was destined to demonstrate God's nature
through his whole countenance. Furthermore, it was common
for a dying patriarch of a family to pass on a prophetic blessing
to each child. These prophetic blessings were considered part of
their inheritance and identity.

Unlike Adam, I did not always feel that my name was a
prophetic blessing, especially regarding my middle name. I was
proud to be the third Robert Hazlett born in my family line, but
I did not enjoy my middle name until I understood its
significance. My middle name belonged my maternal grandfather
whom I never met because he died when my mother was a
young girl. He was a Spirit-filled Methodist lay minister. Several
years ago, my mother gave me his Bible. It was filled sermon
notes and stories of spiritual and prophetic experiences. I
realized his experiences were all part of my inheritance. I have
found that my first, middle, and last names all have spiritual
significance to me, but my middle name was a secret blessing. It
is part of my identity.

Abraham and Sarah were given names from God, too. They
were named Abram and Sarai at birth, and God chose them to

be the patriarchs of the nation of Israel. God encountered them and blessed them with new names which carried a new identities:

> *Abram (pronounced in Hebrew awb-rawm) means high father, while Abraham (pronounced in Hebrew awb-raw-hawm) means father of a multitude. Sarai (pronounced in Hebrew saw-rah-ee) means noble woman, while Sarah (pronounced in Hebrew saw-raw) means princess. As with Abram's name change to Abraham, Sarai's singularly noble name was multiplied in meaning to Sarah.ˣ*

In addition to multiplying the meaning of their names, God also pronounced spiritual blessings on them also. He gave them a middle name that sounded like His. The sound of *Yahweh* is like the sound of breath. Just as He breathed into Adam and Eve, God also breathed on Abram and Sarai. They became "Abra-*ha*-m" and "Sar-*ha*," which sounded like Yahweh or breath. Their names became a sound of heaven that would impact the earth.

After giving new identity, God also placed a prophetic blessing on Abraham:

> *I will make you into a great nation, and I will bless you; I will make your name great, and you will be a blessing. I will bless those who bless you, and whoever curses you I will curse; and all peoples on earth will be blessed through you.*
> *~ Genesis 12:2-3 (NKJV)*

Again echoing Adam and Eve's experience with God, the prophetic blessing on Abraham and Sarah promised a three-fold impact: increase ("I will make you a great nation"), influence ("I will make your name great"), and inheritance ("all peoples of the earth will be blessed through you").

Prophecy is the gift that keeps on giving. Though Abraham was given that blessing thousands of years ago, I am directly impacted as his prophetic blessing continues to be fulfilled today. His increase becomes my increase, his influence strengthens my influence, and I share in His inheritance.

 @bob_hazlett

The purpose of the prophetic and hearing God's voice is not only to find out what God wants to do but to reconnect people with who God is.

The prophetic blessings spoken to me in Pensacola, Florida, were not just for me; they were for all those I would one day impact as well. Your promises, likewise, connect you to others. In some sense, prophecy connects us all with God's plans and promises. We were all chosen in Christ before the foundation of the world. Prophecy connects us to who we are in Christ today. As Paul said in 1 Corinthians 15:22 (NIV), "For as in Adam all die, so in Christ all will be made alive." In Christ, we are connected!

The Sound of God in the Season of the Day

Genesis describes God's daily interaction with man as "the sound of the Lord God as He was walking in the garden in the cool of the day" (Gen. 3:8, NIV). As we have learned, God's sound can be a whisper as with Elijah or it can be a roar as with David. But we can be sure of this: when God comes on the scene, there is a sound released. The cool of the day can also be translated as "the season of the day." The atmosphere or the season that God is ushering in determines the sound of God.

When God first encountered man in the garden, He spoke a name that gave them identity and then a blessing that brought increase, influence, and inheritance. In Genesis 3, after man sinned, man had ushered in a new season, and God entered that season with His sound. The sound of the Lord in the cool of the day was not as encouraging as the first time He spoke: His words told them increase would only come with great pain and labor, influence would be limited, and their inheritance would be death:

> *"I will make your pains in childbearing very severe; with painful labor you will give birth to children. Your desire will be for your husband, and he will rule over you." To Adam he said, "Because you listened to your wife and ate fruit from the tree about which I commanded you, 'You must not eat from it,' Cursed is the ground because of you; through painful toil you will eat food from it all the days of your life. It will produce thorns and thistles for you, and you will eat the plants of the field. By the sweat of your brow you will eat your food until you return to the ground, since from it you were taken; for dust you are and to dust you will return."*
>
> *~ Genesis 3:16-19 (NIV)*

Humanity was utterly lost. The wonderful news is that Jesus came to seek and save that which was lost. He came to restore the prophetic blessing to man and the earth. He came with a new sound.

I believe God is bringing a new sound into the earth. It is the sound of a generation that has walked with God in the cool of the day. They have heard the sound of deep calling unto deep. They have felt the roar of the waterfall. The have sung the song of the redeemed. A new generation with a new voice, they have heard the whisper and the roar. They will be a generation with a new prophetic sound, connected to God and to one another. They will be God's sound in a raging world. Get ready to hear the roar!

CHAPTER 9
PRACTICING GOD'S SOUND

"Some books claiming to be exhaustive are only
exhausting to read."

—A.W. Tozer, Preparing for Jesus' Return:
Daily Live the Blessed Hope

Practicing God's Sound

Over the years, through many of my own experiences, I have learned some tips to help you see through see God's breath on people and speak it into being. God's sound comes in many ways. At times people are overwhelmed when they begin a journey in pursuing prophetic ministry. In order to demystify God's voice a bit, I've compiled some simple tips to help you hear God for others and share those words in a spirit of love.

 @bob_hazlett

The ability to laugh at a mistake shows a willingness to take ownership of it. It also shows an unwillingness to repeat it!

Many of the tips included in this chapter are previously discussed in the book but expounded upon a little more here. Feel free to use this chapter as a quick reference, a go-to guide for tools to equip you in beginning a learning journey with the Holy Spirit. We want to *ra'ah* when we look at people, and here are some pointers to facilitate in that journey.

Tip #1: Learn to See through the Eyes of Your Heart

In Ephesians 1:17-18 (NIV), Paul tells us,

> *I keep asking that the God of our Lord Jesus Christ, the glorious Father, may give you the Spirit of wisdom and revelation, so that you may know him better. I pray that the eyes of your heart may be enlightened in order that you may know the hope to which he has called you.*

The way you see what is temporal is through the eyes in your head. They way you see what is eternal is through the eyes of your heart. The word used here in Ephesians for "eyes of your heart" can also be translated as deep thought or imagination.

We have all been given an imagination. We use it all the time. Worry is imagining the worst, and hope is imagining the best. The eyes of your heart will be used all the time in prophetic ministry. At times, what I would call a vision just seems like something I'm imagining in my own mind. However, when God uses your imagination, there is nothing pretend about it. The eyes of your heart allow you to look past what you can see in the physical to God's amazing design in the spiritual.

Our imaginations can become tainted. We are exposed to so many visual images, and many of them are not godly. The Bible says that the pure in heart will see God (Matt. 5:8). It may be helpful to cleanse your imagination by being mindful of what you allow your eyes to view. Just as fasting food can cleanse your body, you may choose to fast some form of entertainment or technology. Ask the Holy Spirit to guide you in this, and He may show you things you can do to cleanse your imagination so you can see clearer than ever before. When the eyes of your heart are enlightened, you can see what God sees. When you see what God sees, you can say what God says.

 @bob_hazlett

If you feel like you haven't heard God speak lately, remember, conversations are two-way communication. Ask and it will be given.

Tip #2: Learn to Watch for Prophetic Signs

God loves to talk. The problem is, must of us were raised in a culture which subconsciously taught us that supernatural communication is impossible or silly; therefore, we never learned to develop our spiritual senses to observe such occurrences. God speaks all the time, but we must train our senses to discern when God is speaking. A quick study of the Bible will show that God speaks in a myriad of impossibly creative ways: through nature, dreams, miracles, sounds, and even mundane, everyday objects. These things are often intended by God to be signs for us, offering direction or confirmation. We tend to overlook signs because we often don't know what to look for. Here are three tips for hearing God's sound through signs.

1. Pay Attention

   A sign points to something, but if you miss the sign, you miss the point. There arc three common types of signs that you can look for.

   a. *Repetition:* God emphasizes something repeatedly. For example, if you are seeing the same number or hearing the same phrase over and over, God may be speaking to you.

   b. *Unusual setting:* Something appears in an abnormal context. God may draw your attention to something that seems out of place just so He can speak to you about it. Also, pay attention to things that catch your attention for no apparent reason.

   c. *Miraculous appearance:* A "God-thing" happens which points to something. Don't downplay God's activity as mere coincidences. That really weird thing that happened to you earlier today may be God speaking to you through unusual, miraculous circumstances.

2. Respond with intention

   Start a dialogue with the Holy Spirit. Signs are meant to direct you to Him, so let Him lead you in the interpretation of the signs as well. Signs make you wonder, so ask lots of questions, such as these:

    a. *What is the sign pointing me to?*

    b. *What does it mean to me?*

    c. *What should I do as a result?*

3. Respond with action

    Sometimes God speaks through signs just because He's a talking God who loves to bring us into conversation. However, most often signs are given because you will need to take bold action. That boldness can take several forms.

    a. *Bold faith*: A sign helps you believe God is with you when it feels He is not.

    b. *Bold obedience:* A sign helps you do something that seems risky or dangerous.

    c. *Bold declaration:* A sign backs up a bold declaration that God will tell you to make.

Tip #3: Learn How to Share a Destiny Word

At the core of prophetic ministry is hearing what God is saying for others and telling them about it. However, that can be a daunting task for some people. Many people struggle less with *hearing* God's heart for others and more with knowing how and when to *share* what they have heard. Here are some simple guidelines for how to share God-inspired words and put a smile on someone's face.

1. Keep it short: When God was naming something that would be an eternal symbol of what light represents, He kept it short: "day." It is something we wake up to every

day—something we define the length of our lives by—and He made it simple. When identifying God's breath in someone, try to find a word or short phrase that identifies them. For example, say, "you are . . ." courageous, faithful, caring, funny, and so on. Every prophecy starts with a word. Make it a powerful one!

2. Keep it positive: Prophecy is identifying what people are, not what they are not. I have never bought a product because of what it is not. I have never watched a movie because of who was not acting in it. When we tell people what they can be, we empower them to become it.

3. Paint a picture: Ask God to show what the person looks like in the environment that God intends them to live in. Put them in that environment. For example, if you started by saying, "You are caring," ask God to show you the environment in which they are caring. "I see you caring for children in a school." As you start simple, ask God to show you bit by bit more of the picture. As you are faithful to share the little, He will train you to see the more.

4. Fill in the gaps with destiny: Ask God to show you His breath on different areas of their lives, perhaps an area where it has not been clearly displayed. If God stamped them "caring," then that stamp should show up everywhere. Ask God to show you new areas He wants to expand His breath in their lives. For example, "Sometimes your family doesn't see how much you care, but God wants to thank you for caring for your siblings when they were younger. God is going to help you care for your family now."

5. Be creative: God does not make copies, only originals. God may stamp us with similar characteristics, but they will display uniquely through us. When we are learning how God speaks, we should develop comfortable phrases to get started. I like to say, "Can I tell you something that will make you smile?" Some people say, "God loves you and has a plan for your life." This is a good starting practice. In Genesis, we hear God say, "Let there be" over and over, and then He speaks specifically. It's OK to start out generally, but you need to learn to get specific. God is creative and created everyone uniquely. Try different techniques and see what works well for you.

Tip #4: Always Speak Hope, Never Criticism

I'm often asked the question, "Why do I see problems when I ask God to speak to me about other people?" I hate clichés but one is appropriate here: What would Jesus do? What do we see God doing in Genesis 1? The earth was a total wreck—dark, formless, and empty. Instead of pointing out the obvious need, He speaks His desires and purposes into existence. We must learn to do the same.

There are three reasons why we might see something negative over someone. First, we are seeing it because it is there. Just because we see something doesn't mean we have to do anything about it. Take a look at your surroundings and see if you can identify an object that you hadn't noticed was there before. Even though it's there, you don't have to do anything about it. Likewise, when we see people, we may see a whole mixed bag of their outward appearance, their demeanor, their emotional state, as well as God's destiny. Our job isn't to address every single thing we see. Our job is to identify God's life-giving words and share those. If you notice things that are negative, stay away from them. It's not your jurisdiction! Just because you have been given eyes to see doesn't mean you are supposed to speak out the negative things you notice. God's words bring the solution rather than pointing out the problems.

 @bob_hazlett

I find that people need and appreciate encouragement, even if they are not having a bad day. Who says you can't make a good day better!

Second, you may be seeing negative things because God is asking you to pray for them. Humbly keep those concerns before God in prayer and allow Him to lead the person according to His desires. If you are in relationship with that person, God may give you permission to address the concerns in kindness, thoughtfulness, and humility. Any words of correction are always to be shared within the over-arching context of God's amazing destiny and plans for the person's life.

Third, you may be seeing negative things because you are seeing the enemy's plans. In that case, flip it! Don't be afraid or make Satan's schemes out to be bigger than God's amazing destiny. Ask God what He is doing about what you see, and speak life and provision over those circumstances.

My wife has a saying she uses with our kids many times, "Use your life words." She says it in her sweet "mom" voice when one of the children gets verbally out of line, and it's a reminder that our words should be used to speak life and destiny over others. She must use it a lot because one time I was driving with my children in the back seat and someone cut me off in traffic. I started saying, "That person needs to . . . " when a duet from the back seat cut me off.

"Use your life words, dad!" It was a good reminder from the word cops in the back seat to always speak hope and never criticism.

Tip #5: Desire to Help Others Grow

When we do have negative or corrective words for people, our desire should always be to help people grow. Rather than pointing out the negative, we challenge people to live up to their God-designed potentials. I love the correction of God in my personal life. I need it so I can grow up. Hebrews 12 tells us that God disciplines us as sons. Sometimes God does speak corrective words to us, but please remember that the most effective discipline and correction is done within the context of relationship. Relationship gives you the right to be heard.

If you feel that you need to give words of correction or discipline, please weigh these two considerations before sharing the words. First, learn to receive loving correction from God; know that He is your Father and wants you to become all He created you to be. It is only through an attitude of humility that corrective words can be received. Second, realize that correction will be best received when you are in proper relationship with the person and you have earned the right to be heard. These two things have helped me.

I am not afraid or ashamed of the corrective nature of prophetic ministry. Jesus is the Truth, and He is my best friend. If I saw someone driving down a one-way street traveling in the wrong direction, I would correct the person. I am not a traffic cop, but I want them and the others on that street to live long, happy lives.

Ephesians 4 tells us that one of the gifts to the church is the prophet, and one of the gifts of the prophet is to speak the truth in love that we may grow up in all things into Him (Eph. 4:15). When truth is spoken in love, it builds people up so they become mature. Truth spoken without love can have the opposite effect by tearing down or stunting growth. The primary purpose of prophetic ministry, according to Ephesians 4, is not speaking truth; it is helping people grow into all things they are created to be in Christ. The process by which we do that often includes speaking truth in love, but speaking truth is always secondary to helping them grow. If we value prophecy more than we value people, we may not be benefitting their wellbeing. Our primary goal in bringing correction through truth should be to bring people to maturity so they can live a long and happy life.

Tip #6: Don't Fret over "Is It God or Me?"

One of the most frequent questions I hear is, "When I try to hear God speak, I wonder if it is God or me. How can I tell the difference?" This is a wonderful question, and it is a testimony that the person wants to please God and to be careful only to speak His words. However, I believe the question is unnecessary; it's always *both* God and me. Even when we miss it big and it is "just me," He is the one who helps discern that.

Religion requires perfection, but the kingdom values excellence. If we strive for perfection and don't allow ourselves room to be wrong, we will never grow. Perfection is an unattainable destination, but excellence is an exciting journey. It's a journey in which we allow the Holy Spirit to teach, guide, and mentor us. If you strive to never make a mistake, you will make the biggest one by never stepping out in faith.

There are several gauges we can utilize to help us determine if it is God or me. First, use the scripture test. Ask yourself if the word you think you heard from God aligns with scripture. If not, you are either misinterpreting what you heard, or you are misapplying the message. Second, use the Spirit test. Does the word seem good to the Holy Spirit and to you? If what you hear grieves you or the Holy Spirit in you, re-evaluate the message or how you plan to say it. Third, use the confirmation test. Does what you hear align with what God has already spoken? God will not contradict Himself. We may not always understand the implications or details of God's words, but they will never contradict each other.

If you are uncertain, try asking a question rather than making a statement. If you feel like God is telling you about someone's daughter, it would be best to first ask if they have a daughter. If they don't, you either misheard or misinterpreted what you heard.

Always approach prophetic ministry with humility. God resists the proud but gives grace to the humble. If you walk in humility and get a prophetic word right, you won't let it go to your head and God will get the glory. If you walk in humility and miss it, you won't beat yourself up and quit because God will give you grace. If you do miss it, God's grace is big enough both to cover you and to minister to the other person. The key is to learn from your mistakes so that you become better at hearing God in the future.

Tip #7: Keep Practicing and Never Give Up

No new skill comes easy at first. Babies fall many times before they are able to successfully walk. Being certain of God's voice becomes easier with practice. The more I spend time in the Bible, the clearer His voice is to me. The more I step out and share a word, the easier it is to try it again the next time. Never give up. This is your destiny! Don't allow discouragement to persuade you away from the truth that God speaks to you and desires to speak through you.

Also, there will be learning experiences, both positive and negative. God uses both to move us forward in growth. Don't allow those challenges to rob you of God's calling. If you find yourself stuck, speak with the Holy Spirit and allow Him to comfort and instruct you through relationship. As you continue on in the journey to partner with God in the supernatural, you will experience some failures. Not every sick person will be healed. Not every prophetic word will hit the mark exactly or be received. If we base our motivation for today's risks on yesterday's successes or failures, we will never step out. However, if we risk today because we know we have a God who loves people, we can never fail. Love wins!

What an exciting journey we have been invited on! God's sound reverberates through the raging world. He could speak His purposes into existence on His own, but He loves us too much to leave us out of the fun. As sons and daughters of God, He brings us alongside Him to continue to release His love, purposes, and destiny all over the earth. Never give up. The roar can't be silenced. Make the choice to take a chance, step out in risk, and join God on this exciting adventure of relationship with a roaring God.

Endnotes

[i] Moses Maimonides, *The Guide for the Perplexed,* trans. M. Friedlander, 1904; *Teach It to Me,* Sept. 5, 2004, accessed July 21, 2013, ch. 5, http://www.teachittome.com/seforim2/seforim/the_guide_for_the_perplexed.pdf.

[ii] "Entropy and the Second Law," Andrew Duffy, *Physics 105, Boston University Class Pages,* posted Dec 12, 1999, accessed July 21, 2013, http://physics.bu.edu/~duffy/py105/Secondlaw.html.

[iii] "Revelation," *The Free Online Dictionary by Farlex,* last updated 2009, accessed July 21, 2013, http://www.thefreedictionary.com/revelation.

[iv] Malcolm Gladwell, *Outliers: The Story of Success* (New York: Hachette, 2008) 39.

[v] "The Ten Plagues of Egypt," *Creation Ministries International,* accessed July 21, 2013, http://creation.com/the-ten-plagues-of-egypt.

[vi] Moses Maimonides, ch. 5.

[vii] Moses Maimonides, ch. 36.

[viii] James F. Collins, "TF Translates DNA into Music Sequence," *The Harvard Crimson,* April 26, 2007, accessed July 19, 2013, http://www.thecrimson.com/article/2007/4/26/tf-translates-dna-into-music-sequence/.

[ix] *Your DNA Song,* 2012, accessed July 19, 2013, www.yourdnasong.com.

[x] Wayne Blank, "Abram and Sarai," *Daily Bible Study,* March 10, 2013, accessed July 21, 2013, http://www.keyway.ca/htm2006/20060520.htm.